OECD Studies on SMEs and Entrepreneurship

Entrepreneurship in Regional Innovation Clusters

CASE STUDY OF CHIANG MAI AND CHIANG RAI, THAILAND

OECD
BETTER POLICIES FOR BETTER LIVES

This document, as well as any data and map included herein, are without prejudice to the status of or sovereignty over any territory, to the delimitation of international frontiers and boundaries and to the name of any territory, city or area.

Please cite this publication as:
OECD (2021), *Entrepreneurship in Regional Innovation Clusters: Case Study of Chiang Mai and Chiang Rai, Thailand*, OECD Studies on SMEs and Entrepreneurship, OECD Publishing, Paris, *https://doi.org/10.1787/2a24a552-en*.

ISBN 978-92-64-74485-1 (print)
ISBN 978-92-64-18458-9 (pdf)

OECD Studies on SMEs and Entrepreneurship
ISSN 2078-0982 (print)
ISSN 2078-0990 (online)

Photo credits: Cover © PhotoAlto/Getty Images, © David Wasserman/Brand X Pictures/Getty Images, © Tim Pannell/Corbis, © Andersen Ross/Photodisc/Getty Images.

Corrigenda to publications may be found on line at: *www.oecd.org/about/publishing/corrigenda.htm*.

Foreword

This report examines how to develop SME and entrepreneurship policy in Thailand to strengthen Thailand's regional innovation clusters and the sectors that will act as engines for Thailand's future growth. In particular, it examines the policy developments needed to strengthen the innovation cluster in Chiang Mai and Chiang Rai in the North of Thailand, built around the advanced agriculture and biotechnology and food-for-the-future sectors, and draws broader lessons for Thai SME and entrepreneurship policy.

National public research and development (R&D) activities in biotechnology are delivering R&D-based innovations with high commercialisation potential in advanced agriculture and biotechnology and food-for-the-future. However, there is insufficient exploitation of these technologies by Thai enterprises. A shift is therefore needed in Thai SME and entrepreneurship support towards deeper and more targeted finance and advice for existing and potential start-ups and scale-ups with high potential to integrate R&D-based technologies in their products and reach out to international markets.

To make that shift, this report recommends introducing a range of new SME and entrepreneurship policies. It argues that measures are needed to strengthen skills, ease access to financing and overcome barriers in regulation within the Chiang Mai and Chiang Rai regional entrepreneurial ecosystem. It calls for the introduction of a new "fast track" stream of business development services alongside existing basic generic business advice for the regional innovation cluster. This "fast track" support stream would be aimed at high-growth potential start-ups and scale-ups in regional innovation clusters. It would offer more intensive, specialised and higher-quality support than currently available for the typical SME. The report also calls for the creation of a regional cluster management organisation to co-ordinate a range of networking and collaboration projects in Chiang Mai and Chiang Rai with an emphasis on supporting the introduction of technological innovations in potential start-ups and scale-ups through linkages with science parks, universities and research organisations. As well as supporting development in Chiang Mai and Chiang Rai, these measures can be rolled out more widely across Thailand's potential future growth sectors. The Office of Small and Medium-Sized Enterprise Promotion (OSMEP) has a key role to play in this agenda, in partnership with other government ministries and agencies.

Acknowledgements

This report was prepared by the Centre for Entrepreneurship, SMEs, Regions and Cities (CFE) of the Organisation for Economic Co-operation and Development (OECD), led by Lamia Kamal-Chaoui, Director, at the request of the Office of Small and Medium Enterprise Promotion (OSMEP) of the Government of Thailand. The project forms part of the OECD Thailand Country Programme and supports the activities of the OECD Local Employment and Economic Development Committee on local clusters, industrial transition and emerging industries and the OECD Committee on SMEs and Entrepreneurship on entrepreneurial ecosystems and the spatial dimension of entrepreneurship performance.

The project was led by Dr. Jonathan Potter, Head of the Entrepreneurship Policy and Analysis Unit, CFE, OECD, who also edited the report. The report was drafted by the following team: Thanchanok Suwanprasert and Wichai Limpitikranon (Kenan Foundation Asia – focus on the regional economy), Helen Lawton Smith (Birkbeck, University of London – focus on the regional entrepreneurial ecosystem), Lois Stevenson (consultant, Canada – focus on business development services), Dimitris Assimakopoulos (EM Lyon, France – focus on foreign direct investment and SME linkages) and Bjorn Asheim (University of Stavanger, Norway – focus on clusters and new path development).

Project co-ordination support and report comments were provided by Wimonkan Kosumas, Wittawat Lamsam, Vorapoj Prasanpanich, and Wipasirin Wisuthakul of the OSMEP, Thailand. Many other individuals and organisations in Thailand provided important information and comments for the report. A wide range of stakeholders participated in meetings with the OECD review panel during an OECD study mission to Bangkok, Chiang Mai and Chiang Rai in July 2019. Several ministries and government ministries provided comments on the draft report.

Comments were also provided by Karen Maguire, Head of the Local Employment and Social Innovation Division at OECD CFE.

Acronyms and abbreviations

ABDSI	Association of Business Development Services Indonesia
AME	Institute for Advanced Manufacturing and Engineering
ARDA	Agricultural Research Development Agency
ASEAN	Association of Southeast Asian Nations
BDS	Business Development Services
BDSP	Business Development Service Provider
BIOTEC	National Centre for Genetic Engineering and Biotechnology
BOI	Board of Investment
BSC	Business Service Centre
CAD	Canadian Dollar
CEO	Chief Executive Officer
CFE	Centre for Entrepreneurship, SMEs, Regions and Cities
CMO	Cluster Management Organisation
CMU	Chiang Mai University
CWLEP	Coventry and Warwickshire Local Enterprise Partnership
DBD	Department of Business Development
DEPA	Digital Economy Promotion Agency
DIP	Department of Industrial Promotion
DITP	Department of International Trade Promotion
DIW	Department of Work
DOA	Department of Agriculture
EEDA	East of England Development Agency
ERBI	Eastern Region Biotechnology Initiative
ERP	Enterprise Resource Planning
EUR	Euro
FDA	Food and Drug Administration
FDI	Foreign Direct Investment

FIN	Food Innovation and Packaging Centre
FTI	Federation of Thai Industries
GBP	Great Britain Pound
GDP	Gross Domestic Product
GEM	Global Entrepreneurship Monitor
HEI	Higher Education Institution
HEFCE	Higher Education Funding Council for England
ICT	Information and Communication Technology
IoT	Internet of Things
IP	Intellectual Property
ISMED	Institute for Small and Medium Enterprises Development
ISP	Innovation Service Provider
ITAP	Industrial Technology Assistant Programme
JICA	Japan International Cooperation Agency
KET	Key Enabling Technology
KPI	Key Performance Indicator
KSU	Polish National SME Services Network
LBN	London Bioscience Network
LEED	Local Economic and Employment Development
LEO	Local Enterprise Office
MBA	Master of Business Administration
MFii	Mae Fah Luang University Intellectual Property Management and Innovation Department
MFU	Mae Fah Luang University
MFUBI	Mae Fah Luang University Business Incubator
MJU	Mae Jo University
MJUBI	Mae Jo University Business Incubator
MNE	Multinational Enterprise
MOAC	Ministry of Agriculture and Cooperatives
MOC	Ministry of Commerce
MOCSME	Ministry of Cooperatives and SMEs
METI	Ministry of Economy, Trade and Industry (Japan)
MOE	Ministry of Education
MOI	Ministry of Industry
MOST	Ministry of Science and Technology

MOU	Memorandum of Understanding
NAIT	National Agency for Industry and Trade
NCE	Norwegian Centre of Expertise
NECTEC	National Electronics and Computer Technology Centre
N-HIP	Northern Herb Innovation Park
NIA	National Innovation Agency
NIST	Northern Innovative Start-up Thailand
NSP	Northern Science Park
NSTDA	National Science and Technology Development Agency
OECD	Organisation for Economic Co-operation and Development
OHEC	Office of the Higher Education Commission
OSMEP	Office of Small and Medium Enterprises Promotion
OSS	One-Stop Service Centre
PARP	Polish Enterprise Development Agency
R&D	Research and Development
R&D&I	Research and Development and Innovation
RDA	Regional Development Agency
RIC	Regional Innovation Cluster
RISMEP	Regional Integrated SME Promotion
SBA	Small Business Administration
SBIR	Small Business Innovation Research programme
SBDC	Small Business Development Centre
SCC	Startup Canada Communities
SCORE	Service Corps of Retired Executives
SEZ	Special Economic Zone
SME	Small and Medium-sized Enterprise
SMED	Small and Medium Enterprise Development Bank
SMEDI	Small and Medium Enterprises Development Institute
SSRC	SME Support and Rescue Centre
STeP	Science and Technology Park, Chiang Mai University
STTR	Small Business Technology Transfer programme
TCC	Thai Chamber of Commerce
TCELS	Thailand Centre of Excellence for Life Sciences
TEA	Total Early-stage Entrepreneurial Activity
THAI-BISPA	Thai Business Incubator and Science Park Association

THB	Thai Baht
TCG	Thai Credit Guarantee Corporation
TFV	Thailand Food Valley
TMC	Technology Management Centre
UBI	University Business Incubator
UMG	Unipart Manufacturing Group
USD	United States Dollar

Table of contents

Tables

Boxes

Executive summary

This report examines how to strengthen regional innovation clusters and sectors driving future growth in Thailand by stimulating innovative start-ups and scale-ups. It explores the case of the advanced agriculture and biotechnology and food-for-the-future cluster in the Chiang Mai and Chiang Rai regions in northern Thailand. However, it also has important lessons for the development of a new generation of SME and entrepreneurship policies for all the future driving sectors in the Thai economy, as Thailand seeks a shift to a more innovation-based small business economy in the post-COVID-19 recovery.

Key messages

The report's main messages are that the Thai government should introduce:

1. **A new "Fast Track" strand of SME support for firms with growth potential**. This could provide specialised and high-quality advice, finance and innovation assistance to start-ups and scale-ups in Thailand's driving sectors of future growth, where these firms have high potential to integrate new technology in their products and to export.
2. **A regional innovation clusters policy**. This could create overarching regional cluster management organisations and cluster management agents in driving sectors for future growth, which would connect start-ups and scale-ups to sources of technology and business development knowledge in universities, public research institutions, science parks and incubators at regional, national and international levels.

The benefits would be to:

- Overcome a bottleneck in the innovation systems of Thailand's driving sectors of future growth concerning limited exploitation of the results of public investments in research and development (R&D) by domestic firms.
- Spread innovation through the exploitation of national R&D results more widely across the regions of Thailand.

The report starts by assessing the economic activities, anchor institutions and policy support mechanisms that support the advanced agriculture and biotechnology and food-for-the-future cluster in Chiang Mai and Chiang Rai. The following chapters examine strengths and weaknesses in the regional entrepreneurial ecosystem for start-ups and scale-ups; business development services; the attraction and embedding of foreign direct investment (FDI); and future industrial path development opportunities in the cluster.

Key findings

There is strong potential for high value-added growth in the advanced agriculture and biotechnology sector and food-for-the-future sectors in Thailand. These are both potential future driving sectors of the

Thai economy, prioritised by the Thailand 4.0 Strategy. Successful development can be driven by Thailand's strong and successful investments in public R&D in biotechnology directed towards discovering products and processes that can add value to existing agricultural production capacities in market niches with growing international demand. Key areas of potential include healthy, medicinal and functional foods and cosmetics. However, the exploitation of R&D results in the market is held back by limited numbers of start-up and scale-up enterprises involved in innovation and exporting in these fields.

A key thrust of Thailand's approach to address the R&D exploitation bottleneck in advanced agriculture and biotechnology and food-for-the-future, and in the other priority sectors in the Thailand 4.0 Strategy, should be making connections between universities, science parks and research organisations and existing and potential start-ups and scale-ups and building up the absorptive capacity of these firms.

Together, Chiang Mai and Chiang Rai are a potential regional stronghold in Thailand in advanced agriculture and biotechnology and food-for-the-future products. They have substantial agricultural production in rice, fruits, vegetables and organic products where value can be added by incorporating biotechnology innovations. They also have regional universities and science parks working actively in biotechnology and related research, which can provide industry with access to public research results. However, more support is needed to provide the right growth-oriented finance and advice to potential and existing start-ups and scale-ups, and to create the right links to relevant innovation sources.

These policies need to address the following issues:

- *Finance.* Private equity, angel investing and venture capital funding are still in the nascent stage. Government support programmes largely emphasise traditional debt finance and are insufficiently targeted on innovative start-ups and scale-ups.
- *Skills.* There are skills shortages in business and innovation management and untapped opportunities for ambitious entrepreneurship among women and university graduates.
- *Regulations.* A lack of standardisation and delays in health product licensing are a barrier for start-ups and scale-ups to exploit new biotechnology-based products.
- *Business advice.* Existing government-supported business advice is modelled on basic services for the typical micro firm and not sufficiently deep for innovative start-ups and scale-ups. Technology development advice is not well integrated with business development advice in complementary areas for company development including marketing and management strategy.
- *Foreign direct investment.* Chiang Mai and Chiang Rai have yet to attract significant FDI and few relationships have been created between the existing FDI operations and regional SME suppliers or research institutions.
- *Cluster support.* Despite having several small-scale networks of local firms (including Food Valley) and tax incentives for R&D investments in advanced agriculture and biotechnology and food-for-the-future (through Food Innopolis), Chiang Mai and Chiang Rai lack a unified regional cluster management organisation with associated funding for cluster management agents, cluster development projects and cluster network building.

Key recommendations

This report contains many concrete policy recommendations illustrated by international examples of inspiring policy practices. The following are among the report recommendations:

Build the regional entrepreneurial ecosystem

- Strengthen growth finance for start-ups and scale-ups in the cluster by increasing the targeting of finance programmes to firms with innovation and growth potential, promoting a crowdfunding initiative, and developing a business angel network.
- Introduce sustained funding of university-level entrepreneurship education and start-up support.

Upgrade business development services

- Introduce business development vouchers for high-potential start-ups and scale-ups in the cluster to access intensive, specialised and high-quality private sector consultancy and mentoring for technology integration and internationalisation.
- Scout for SMEs with potential to innovate, grow and export in the cluster and assign them a business development services account manager.

Strengthen institutional arrangements for FDI

- Build and market the regional conditions that will attract FDI in advanced agricultural products to the cluster.
- Introduce systematic FDI aftercare to build links between attracted FDI and regional SMEs, universities, science parks and incubators.

Create a cluster management organisation and cluster management agents

- Create an overarching regional cluster management organisation for the advanced agriculture and biotechnology and food-for-the-future cluster in Chiang Mai and Chiang Rai to support networking, cluster visibility and cluster strategy development.
- Engage cluster management agents to identify high potential start-ups and scale-ups and support them to integrate scientific, engineering and marketing knowledge as well as to co-ordinate a number of strategic cluster projects, including applied R&D projects with regional universities and science parks and training programmes for employees.

1 The Chiang Mai and Chiang Rai economy

This chapter analyses the regional economic context for the development of start-ups and scale-ups in the advanced agriculture and biotechnology sector and the food-for-the-future sector in the Chiang Mai and Chiang Rai regions in Thailand. It provides information on the regional industry sector specialisations, characteristics of the regional entrepreneurial ecosystem, including its anchor institutions such as universities, and the government support policies for SMEs and entrepreneurship in the regions. The chapter makes recommendations on strengthening approaches to the implementation of SME and entrepreneurship policy in the regions.

Introduction

The government's medium-term Thailand Industrial Development Strategy 4.0 targets ten "s-curve" industries with the aim of developing a more innovative and high value added economy, applying technology and innovation to increase the GDP growth rate and per capita income levels. The s-curve industries are: advanced agriculture[1] and biotechnology[2]; smart electronics; food-for-the-future; medical tourism; next-generation automotive; aviation and logistics; biofuels and biochemical; digital economy, automation and robotics; and medical services (Asawachintachit, 2018). The strategy targets functional foods, medical foods, food supplements and food innovation in driving forward the advanced agriculture and biotechnology s-curve and the food-for-the-future s-curve (NESDC, 2016a).

The government is investing nationally in basic and applied R&D in advanced agriculture and biotechnology and food-for-the-future as well as in training approximately 9 600 food scientists, researchers, and technicians and 126 600 food experts between 2018 and 2022 (BOI, 2018). It has also put in place a national cluster development policy for advanced agriculture and biotechnology and food-for-the-future.

These policies aim to support greater value added from Thailand's key agricultural production specialisations. Thailand is a major world producer of cassava (it is the 2nd largest producer in the world), palm oil (3rd), sugarcane (4th), tropical fruits (5th), rice (6th), and coconuts (9th) (FAOSTAT, 2017). It is also a leader in natural foods, herbs and spices for medicinal and health purposes.

The policy actions to support R&D and innovation in food need to be aligned with policy actions that support SMEs[3] to exploit the technology developments, including through small firm start-ups and scale-ups. SMEs contribute 42% of Thailand's total GDP (NESDC, 2019) and will be key to extracting value from government R&D and skills investments.

There are strong opportunities for developing start-ups and scale-ups in agriculture and biotechnology and food-for-the-future in the Chiang Mai and Chiang Rai regions in the Northern region of Thailand, building on existing small firm networks and supply chains in these regions, connecting them together within the regions both vertically and horizontally, and connecting them with the underpinning national cluster (BOI, 2015). This chapter investigates the opportunities and the weak links that policy needs to address.

Chiang Rai is located in the northern continental highland, bordering Myanmar to the north and Laos to the east. It is approximately 805 km north of Bangkok and 416 metres above sea level. Chiang Mai is the second largest economy in Thailand and the largest province in the northern region. A statistical snapshot of the Chiang Mai and Chiang Rai regions is given in Table 1.1.

Table 1.1. Chiang Mai and Chiang Rai regions – statistical snapshot 2018 or latest year available

	Chiang Mai	Chiang Rai
Land area (square kilometres)	20 107	11 678
Agricultural land area (square kilometres)	2 937	4 431
Population	1 700 492	1 140 241
GDP (billion THB)	247	108
GDP (billion USD PPP)	19	8
GDP as share of Thailand	1.5%	0.7%
GDP per capita (THB)	145 280	94 319
GDP per capita (USD PPP)	11 420	7 410
GDP per capita as share of Thailand average	61%	40%
Employment	1 039 957	646 379
Registered employees[1]	153 132	48 739
Number of industrial establishments[1]	63	971

Number of newly registered companies[1]	2 668	1 119
Logistics	3rd largest international airport in country	International airport, border trade
Special Economic Zones[2]	Food Innopolis, Science Park, Space Krenovation Park	Maesai, Chaingsan, Chaingkhong
Main business specialisations	Tourism, food processing	Tourism, agriculture, border trade
Main crops	Rice, longan, lychee	Rice, corn, rubber, longhan

Notes: [1] Data are for 2017
[2] Special Economic Zones (SEZ) provide a variety of benefits to SMEs and start-ups. They vary by location, by industry and by the government department that promotes the zone. Incentives might include income tax reduction, foreign worker allowances, waivers on duty and tax imports of machinery and technology, free trade zones and ability for a foreign entity to own land and a majority of shares in a company.
Source: Regional Investment and Economic Centre 1 Chiang Mai, Chiang Mai Provincial Business Development Office; Chiang Mai Provincial Comptroller General, Office of Commercial Affairs Chiang Rai (see www.cgd.go.th, www.chiangmai.nso.go.th).

Economic activities

SME activities

There are approximately 80 000 SMEs in Chiang Mai and 50 000 SMEs in Chiang Rai. The bulk of the enterprises are micro-enterprises with less than 6 persons engaged, and approximately 15-20% have between 21 and 200 persons engaged (Table 1.2).

Table 1.2. Number of establishments and persons engaged in Chiang Mai and Chiang Rai by size of establishment, 2017

	Chiang Mai			Chiang Rai		
Size of establishment (no. persons)	No. establish-ments	No. persons engaged	% persons engaged	No. establish-ments	No. persons engaged	% persons engaged
1-5	74,419	132,262	46.56	48,379	79,074	53.75
6-10	4,955	37,506	13.20	2,533	19,514	14.01
11-15	1,680	21,326	7.51	795	10,274	7.37
16-20	660	11,832	4.17	377	6,924	4.97
21-25	380	8,610	3.03	188	4,341	3.12
26-30	212	5,982	2.11	113	3,290	2.36
31-50	360	13,825	4.87	147	5,959	4.28
51-100	201	13,806	4.86	67	4,649	3.34
101-200	97	13,211	4.65	21	3,076	2.21
More than 200	59	25,700	9.05	5	2,225	1.60
Total	**83,023**	**284,060**	**100.00**	**52,625**	**139,326**	**100.00**

Source: The 2017 Business and Industrial census (Basic Information) Chiang Mai Provincial, National Statistical Office

In total there were some 14 788 manufacturing establishments in Chiang Mai (18% of all establishments) in 2017 and 7 950 in Chiang Rai (15% of all establishments) according to National Statistical Office data. An idea of the sectoral breakdown of these establishments can be gained from more limited data held by the Provincial Offices relating to a subset of the non-micro, i.e. larger, SMEs with minimum equipment and contacts with the Provincial offices. These data indicate that the agriculture, food and beverage industries make up approximately 25% of all industrial enterprises in Chiang Mai and 41% in Chiang Rai (Table 1.3).

Table 1.3. Number of industrial establishments by type of industry, 2017

Type of industry	Chiang Mai	Chiang Rai
Agriculture	4	268
Food	11	130
Beverages	1	5
Textiles	2	1
Wearing apparel	1	3
Leather products	-	1
Wood and wood products	2	16
Furniture	2	43
Paper and paper product	-	11
Printing	-	-
Chemical	1	12
Petrochemical	2	8
Rubber	-	8
Plastic	2	15
Non-metallic	6	150
Metals	-	-
Metal products	1	33
Machinery and equipment	1	16
Electricity	-	7
Transport	10	87
Others	18	157
Total	**63**	**971**

Note: Industrial establishments are factories with at least 5 horsepower or the equivalent of 5 horsepower or having more than 7 employees using machinery
Source: Chiang Mai and Chiang Rai Provincial Offices

There were some 300 registered start-ups in Chiang Mai and Chiang Rai in 2017 (Table 1.4).

Table 1.4. Number of new registered enterprises, 2017

Type of industry	Chiang Mai	Chiang Rai
Agriculture, forestry and fishing	25	20
Mining and quarrying	3	4
Manufacturing	253	56
Electricity, gas, steam and air conditioning supply	4	3
Water supply: sewerage, waste management and remediation activities	2	1
Construction	304	298
Wholesale and retail trade; repair of motor vehicles and motor cycles	835	503
Transportation and storage	60	2
Accommodation and food service activities	277	26
Information and communication	73	48
Financial and insurance activities	40	9
Real estate activities	281	11
Professional, scientific and technical activities	212	46
Administrative and support service activities	133	37
Public administration and defence: compulsory social security	1	26
Education	28	
Human health and social work activities	39	6
Arts, entertainment and recreation	30	6
Other service activities	68	2
Other		17
Total	**2 668**	**1 119**

Note: There are four types of registration – Limited Company, Limited Partnership, Ordinary Partnership, and Public Limited Company
Source: Chiang Mai and Chiang Rai Offices of Commercial Affairs

Agriculture

Chiang Mai and Chiang Rai are highland regions rich in natural resources, with a temperate climate and good access to water. Their main regional crops include rice, fruit (longan, lychee), corn (animal feed), vegetables, herbs and spices, condiments and medicinal plants (OAE, 2019).

The government is supporting efforts to improve the agricultural value chain by focusing on technology and innovation in the following areas:

- Upstream – farming systems, seeding, water, soil and nutrient management, harvesting.
- Midstream – dehydrating, modifying food, packaging, increasing shelf life, food safety.
- Downstream – marketing, distribution.

Opportunities in healthy, functional and medicinal foods

There is a global trend towards healthier foods and foods with medicinal and functional purposes. For example, there is increasing demand for foods that support and improve brain function, digestion, eyesight, heart, blood, skin, bone and joint health as well as antibiotic, anti-aging and nutritional foods for athletes (Krungthai Bank, 2019). Processed and modified hygienic foods are also gaining popularity. These markets can substantially increase the value of the product from agricultural production. For example, the fermenting, cooking and processing of garlic can increase its sale price 50 to 100-fold per kilogram.

An example of adding value to agricultural production using biotechnology in Thailand involves longan production. Thailand is the largest longan exporter in the world, exporting 72% of its production, and 38% of Thailand's total longan production is in Chiang Mai and Chiang Rai (see Box 1.1)

Box 1.1. Longan as a herbal medicine

Longan contains the following active, healthy ingredients: gallic acid, ellagic acid, tannic acid, GABA and corilagin. A number of uses of longan as a herbal medicine have recently been discovered in Chiang Mai and Chiang Rai, often with the support of the Northern Food Valley initiative:

- With the Natural Bev Co., Ltd., Chiang Mai University has researched the use of biotechnology to extract bioactive compounds from longan that assist in sleeping and have anti-aging properties.
- With funding from the Agricultural Research Development Agency (ARDA), research by Honorary Professor Ussani Winitkhetkamnuan, PhD, special lecturer at the Faculty of Medicine at Chiang Mai University, has discovered natural compounds in longan seeds that suppress cartilage enzyme degradation. This has led to the development of products to treat arthritis and chronic myositis conditions using longan seeds.
- A number of product innovations have been developed in Chiang Mai and Chiang Rai using the longan extract 'Longanoid'. These have received numerous awards throughout Asia.
- Research aimed at extracting compounds from longan seeds is ongoing at Chiang Mai University and Rangsit University.
- Mae Fah Luang University and Khon Kaen University are conducting research on combining longan seeds with other herbs to develop medicinal products.

Source: For more information: www.longanoid.com

A second example of adding value to local agricultural production involves the tea industry. A group of SMEs called the Tea Gallery Group in Chiang Mai is fermenting tea known as kombucha, which acts as a laxative and improves digestion and liver functions by removing toxins from the body. Research shows benefits for reducing cholesterol, blood pressure, inflammation, migraines and fatigue.

A number of business start-ups in Chiang Mai and Chiang Rai have developed by using biotechnology to produce higher value, healthy foods. Examples are:

- Sleep Well, which produces beverages that aid sleep using vanilla and honey;
- Tofusun, which produces milk from soybeans fortified with melatonin to aid sleep;
- Morinaga, which produces a candy with lactic acid bacteria to prevent the common cold; and
- Juiceinnov8, which produces fruit juice with reduced natural sugars to help prevent diabetes.

There is potential for further development of start-ups and scale ups based on new biotechnology-based products in Chiang Mai and Chiang Rai in the food and cosmetics sectors.

Anchor institutions

There are several anchor institutions in Chiang Mai and Chiang Rai that can play key roles in supporting the flow of technical knowledge to regional start-ups and scale-ups in advanced agriculture and biotechnology and food-for-the-future. The main anchor institutions are universities, science parks, research institutes and business incubators supported by public policy.

Universities

The universities in Chiang Mai and Chiang Rai support the entrepreneurial ecosystem in several ways. They supply skilled graduates in agriculture, food science, biotechnology, herbal medicine and cosmetics. They also support start-ups and scale-ups through R&D services, laboratory testing, business development support and nurturing start-up ideas. The universities work with start-ups and scale-ups in areas such as Technology Business Incubation, collaborative research, intellectual property and innovative design, and offering workshops and seminars on new technologies.

Chiang Mai University

Chiang Mai University is a public research university with approximately 35 000 students and a strong emphasis on engineering, science, agriculture, and medicine. As well as specialisations in aviation and 5G technology it includes activities for business co-operation in advanced agriculture and biotechnology and food-for-the-future.

Among other support, the Faculty of Agro Industry provides education, access to alumni, and seminars on agricultural and packaging design for local businesses and business clusters, the Agricultural Technology Service Centre holds seminars and workshops for local businesses and the Food Innovation and Packaging Centre provides research and food innovation development, including services for product testing and analysis, innovative packaging design and consulting support.

In addition, the Science and Technology Park (STeP) connects the University and the private sector on technology and innovation in the areas of agriculture, food, medicine, biotechnology, IT software, digital content, energy and materials (www.step.cmu.ac.th).

Mae Jo University

Mae Jo University is Thailand's oldest agricultural institution with approximately 15 000 students. Originally established as the Northern Agricultural Teachers Training School under the Ministry of Education, Mae Jo received university status in 1996. It includes a business incubator with a range of services (www.mjubi.mju.ac.th). The incubator offers business education for faculty members, researchers, students, alumni and local business owners. It provides business consulting services to entrepreneurs in business processes, innovation, production, marketing, management and accounting. It also collaborates with firms on research, proof of technology, development and commercialisation. It also manages intellectual property belonging to the University.

Mae Fah Luang University

Mae Fah Luang University was established in 1998 in Chiang Rai in two campuses at Doi Ngam and Mae Suay. The University has 13 000 students and is well regarded for its science, cosmetics and agriculture faculties (www.mfu.ac.th). The University includes a number of facilities that support R&D commercialisation in advanced agriculture and biotechnology and food-for-the-future:

- The *Tea and Coffee Institute* provides education, R&D and technology consulting services on tea and tea products to promote the Thai tea industry to international markets. (http://web2.mfu.ac.th/other/teainstitute/?lang=en)
- The *Centre of Excellence in Natural Product Innovation* provides lab testing services for cosmetic ingredients, *lab* and testing equipment and conducts R&D on natural products. (https://cenpi.mfu.ac.th/home-cenpi.html)
- The *University Business Incubator* provides consulting services to SMEs and start-ups in the *agriculture*, health and cosmetics sectors (but does not offer physical co-location facilities). (http://mfubi.mfu.ac.th)

- The *University Intellectual Property Management and Innovation Department Office serves* as a centre for technology commercialisation and provides design innovation and intellectual property to the private sector. (http://mfii.mfu.ac.th)

Northern Science Park

The Northern Science Park (NSP) is one of three regional science parks in Thailand. It is supported by the Regional Science Park Programme launched by the Science Park Promotion Agency and the Thai Ministry of Science and Technology (MOST) in 2012.

The science park is operated by Chiang Mai University's Science and Technology Park (STeP), which acts as the headquarters of the Northern Science Park project. STeP aims to commercialise research from Chiang Mai University in industries in the region using the triple helix model concept, i.e. innovating through collaboration between the private, academic and government sectors. However, there are six other universities in the Northern region affiliated to NSP: Meajo University, Mae Fah Luang University, University of Phayao, Uttaradit Rajabpat University, Naresuan University and Pibulsongkram Rajabhat University. Since 2012, STeP is also the administrative office for Creative Chiang Mai, a network which seeks to create and support regional innovation ecosystems.

NSP and STeP play key roles in transferring R&D in regional universities to regional start-ups and scale-ups in the Northern Region, mainly focused on innovation in the value chains for agriculture and food, medical and biotechnology, IT software and digital content, and IoT and energy technology (CMU Corporate Relations and Alumni Center, 2018).

In May 2018, NSP opened a new 20 750 square metre building on 22 rai of land in the Mae-Hia campus of Chiang Mai University dedicated to acting as a 'Total Innovation Solution Centre' for SMEs. The site contains R&D laboratories, office space, meeting rooms, co-working spaces, and a 440-seat convention hall. Some 95% of the office units were occupied in August 2019.

There were 35 private sector companies in the NSP in 2019, in the following fields: IT software and digital content (59%), agriculture and food (15%), medical and bio-technology (13%), and energy technology and materials (13%)[4]. Among the companies are:

- Synapes (Thailand) Co., Ltd: A research-based company focusing on artificial intelligence (AI) technologies including cognitive computation, natural language understanding (NLU), machine learning, deep learning, and visual intelligence technologies.
- Horganice Co., Ltd.: A real estate management platform created by a graduate of Chiang Mai University. It manages approximately 3 000 apartments and has clients in all 77 provinces of Thailand.
- Siam Novas Co., Ltd.: A company working on immunology and reproductive research.
- Navis Plus Co., Ltd.: A herbal and natural product supplement manufacturer.
- BuddyGo Co., Ltd.: A digital car rental platform.
- Plastech Corporation: A successful start-up that was nurtured by R&D collaboration with the NSP. It has invented a prototype called the 'Micro PAW System' that uses plasma technology and micro-nano bubbles for dispersing pesticides in fruits and vegetables. It has drawn significant investor interest.

There are also eight public agencies located on the NSP, including the National Innovation Agency (NIA) and the Thailand Centre of Excellence for Life Science. Their main activities include R&D consultancy, technology transfer and public-private sector co-operation.

NSP also provides R&D and business incubator services with the goal of commercialising the research. This includes providing business matching, working space, wet and dry test laboratories, cleanroom laboratories, prototyping and an exhibition hall.

A second phase of the NSP was approved in 2019 with a budget of THB 385 million to develop 7 rai of land between 2020 and 2022. The goal is to further develop the medical, biotechnology, IT software, digital content and energy technology and materials sectors. It is expected to be able to host up to 155 start-ups with an economic value of THB 3.8 billion.

Between 2012 and 2019, NSP supported over 700 SMEs and worked with 140 start-ups, 40 of which are in Chiang Mai. It has been supporting start-ups at a rate of approximately 30 per year. For 2019, for example, its aim was to support at least 100 entrepreneurs with a target success rate of 25 successful start-ups. NSP estimates that the economic value created through these start-up firms is over THB 2 billion. Furthermore, during 8 months of 2019, NSP reports that it had 45 100 visitors from the private sector, universities and the government. It estimated that it had created 108 R&D jobs with private investment of THB 120 million and an economic value of THB 328 million in 2019, and forecasted that by 2024 it will employ 5 640, including 1 636 jobs in R&D, with economic value created of THB 546 million and 700 tech start-ups (Prachachat.net, 2019).

Research institutes

Northern Herb Innovation Park (N-HIP) is located in the NSP. N-HIP is a collaboration with the Pharmaceutical Science faculty at STeP, Chiang Mai University, and the Department of Thai Traditional and Alternative Medicine (under the Ministry of Public Health). It includes the Herbal and Holistic Medicine Total Solution Centre, a research centre opened in March 2018 with the goal of developing the Thai herb industry, including cosmetics, health supplements, heathy beverages and natural medicine.

BIOTEC is a national agency under the National Science and Technology Development Agency (NSTDA) headquartered outside the region in Pathum Thani. It provides R&D and technical services in the agricultural, biomedical and environmental areas to firms throughout the country. One of its facilities is a Biomedical Technology Research Laboratory at Chiang Mai University. NSTDA also launched a national Bio Based Start-up Programme in 2018 to create and support biotechnology technology entrepreneurs.

BIOTEC, NSTDA, and the Department of Thai Traditional and Alternative Medicine have signed a Memorandum of Understanding to promote the medical Thai herb industry. Their goals are to grow the industry to annual revenue of THB 320 billion using R&D, engineering, science, technology and innovation to promote 13 Herbal Cities (recently expanded to 14 provinces). The pilot project will transform raw herbal ingredients into high-quality herbal supplements. Chiang Rai will be the hub for the Northern Region.

Box 1.2. Narah Industry Co. Ltd, Chiang Mai

NARAH is an R&D-based start-up located in Chiang Mai manufacturing Thai herb products. It won the Gold Medal and three special prizes for innovation excellence at the 2017 International Invention and Design Competition held in Hong Kong. NARAH produces a line of herbal teas that aid human health. The products have proven effective in the control of diabetes by lowering blood sugar levels and cholesterol, quickly, safely and effectively.

Source: More information: http://en.narahherb.com/

Business incubators

Each of the universities in Chiang Mai and Chiang Rai has a University Business Incubator supported by the Office of Small and Medium Enterprise Promotion (OSMEP) assisting technology-based start-ups by providing R&D, technology transfer, shared infrastructure and other services. Furthermore, in 2018, three government agencies – the NSTDA, the Office of the Higher Education Commission (OHEC) and the OSMEP – jointly signed a memorandum of understanding to establish the Thai Business Incubator and Science Park Association (THAI-BISPA). The Association serves as a focal point for collaboration, business networking, knowledge sharing, and capacity development across the 60 incubators located in science parks and universities across the country.

Policy support mechanisms

Office of Small and Medium Enterprise Promotion (OSMEP)

The Office of Small and Medium Enterprise Promotion (OSMEP) is a government agency under the Ministry of Industry (MOI) that leads the formulation of policies and strategies to promote SMEs across government and operates a range of programmes offering financial support, training, and consultancy to SMEs. Its main programmes are listed below.

Financial loan assistance programmes:

i. SME Development Loans

The government has allocated THB 20 billion to the OSMEP as a fund for long-term, low interest rate loans at 1% interest to support SMEs in the s-curve industries (future driving sectors of the Thai economy), including advanced agriculture and biotechnology and food-for-the-future. Loans are for a period of up to seven years and up to a value of THB 10 million for SMEs. Repayments are not required during an initial period.

ii. SME Transformation Loan

The government has allocated THB 15 billion to the OSMEP as a fund for long-term, low interest rate loans at 3% to SMEs. Loans are for a period of up to seven years and up to a value of THB 15 million. Repayments are not required during an initial period.

iii. SME Rescue Micro-Enterprise Loans

The government has allocated a fund of THB 2 billion to the OSMEP to support rescue loans of up to THB 1 million for small enterprises and up to THB 200 000 for micro, community and social enterprises. The loans are interest free, and repayments are not required during an initial period.

iv. SME Rescue Non-Performing Loans

The government has allocated THB 1 billion to the OSMEP as a fund to support loans of up to 1 million THB for up to seven years to small enterprises. The loans are interest free and repayments are not required during an initial period.

SME training and seminar programmes:

i. *Start-Up / Early Stage Group*

These training offers teach business principles to start-up/early-stage entrepreneurs to encourage sustainable business development. A diverse group typically attends the training, including students, people with no prior business experience, and those with existing businesses. The OSMEP encourages attendees to register as legal entities in order to widen their business opportunities.

ii. *The Strong and Regular Group*

These trainings emphasise increasing the capacity of existing SME and micro-enterprises to grow and realise their potential through innovation. The OSMEP exposes the group to new opportunities such as gaining access to new markets, partnering with foreign entities via e-commerce, introducing modern export practices, and providing access to state sector markets.

iii. *The Turn-around Group*

This training focuses on SMEs that have encountered difficulties in the course of their growth or are at the end of their business life cycle. The goal is to provide financial and business consulting support in order to develop a business improvement plan.

OSMEP One-Stop Service Centres:

The SME One-Stop Service Centres (OSS) offer information and consultancy support to SMEs and help them to navigate to a range of relevant public programmes.

Board of Investment (BOI)

The BOI aims to promote investment by Thai and overseas enterprises to enhance Thailand's competitiveness and sustainable growth (BOI, 2017). The incentives generally target specific industries in specific locations through policies for Special Economic Zones (SEZs), free trade zones, agro-processing clusters and industrial parks. Tax incentives in these areas include corporate tax reduction, duty and tax exemptions, and tax reductions on importing machinery and technology. In addition, the policy creates more facilitative regulations that enable foreign investors to own land in special economic zones and to have 100% shareholdings in local enterprises.

One of the key support instruments for the development of advanced agriculture and biotechnology and food-for-the-future in Chiang Mai and Chiang Rai is the Food Innopolis SEZ, discussed below. In addition, the BOI has designated Chiang Mai and Chiang Rai, together with Lampang and Lamphun, as a regional Agro-processing Industrial Cluster, one of five in Thailand. The initiative is designed to support agricultural processing activities in fruit, vegetables and herbal products, including measures for infrastructure, public utilities development, water, transportation, IP licensing, R&D, co-operation with local universities, product and packaging design and tax incentives. The tax incentives include a three to eight-year corporate income tax exemption with an additional five years in which there is a 50% reduction in corporate income tax and import duty waivers on machinery (Asawachintachit, 2018).

Food Valley

Thailand Food Valley was set up in 2014 to support SMEs in the advanced agriculture and food industries. It involves a collaboration between the Ministry of Agriculture and Cooperatives (MOAC),

Department of Industrial Work (DIW), Ministry of Science and Technology (MOST), Thai Chamber of Commerce (TCC) and Federation of Thai Industries (FTI). The initiative was modelled on the Food Valley ecosystem in the Netherlands. It aims to create sustainable and innovative start-up and scale-up businesses in co-operation with producers, growers, investors, research institutes and government. Information and consultancy are provided to member companies to improve the value chain, food quality, increase exports, and bring technology and innovation. Marketing and branding are also promoted with the "Thai Kitchen to the World" concept.

The Northern Region is the pilot location for the programme. There are two strands of the programme – Northern Food Valley 1 and Northern Food Valley 2:

- **Northern Food Valley 1**

Areas Covered: Chiang Mai, Mae Hong Sorn, Lumphun, Lumpang.

Command Centre: Chiang Mai.

There are about 400 members of Food Valley 1.

Sub sector in Food Valley 1: Chiang Mai, the City of Coffee.

- **Northern Food Valley 2**

Areas Covered: Chiang Rai, Prayoa, Phrae, Nan.

Command Centre: Chiang Rai.

Sub sector in Food Valley 2: Chiang Rai, the City of Tea .

The aim of Food Valley is to work in collaboration with STeP, Lanna Thai Coffee Development Centre, the Mae Jo Tea Institute and Mae Fah Luang University, to make the Northern region Thailand's leading destination for premium tea and arabica coffee, establishing Chiang Mai as the City of Coffee and Chiang Rai as the City of Tea.

Food Innopolis

Food Innopolis (http://foodinnopolis.or.th/en/about-us/) is a national cluster-based initiative with sites in five regions of the country, each with different specific sector targets. It offers infrastructure, human capital and investment incentives for R&D and innovation in food technologies. It was launched in 2016 as a joint initiative of 35 public agencies, private sector companies and universities.

A key component of Food Innopolis is an SEZ, which offers food industry firms exemptions from income tax for three to eight years with a further five year period of 50% reduction in tax after the exempt period expires, and the possibility of permanent Thai residency status for foreign national industry experts and the ability for foreign enterprises to own land in the zone.

The initiative also involves investment in a range of infrastructures and research capacities and networks. At a national level, the initiative aims to establish a network involving 9 000 Food Factories, 150 Food Research Labs, 20 Pilot Plants, 3 000 researchers and 10 000 students across 70 universities.

Food Innopolis is developing projects with three universities in Chiang Mai and Chiang Rai, namely Chiang Mai University on Healthy and Functional Food, Mae Jo University on Organic Food and Mae Fah Luang University on Tea Innovation. It also works with Naresuan University on Herbal Innovation in Phitsanulok Province of Northern Thailand.

Food Innopolis is also expanding to work with three regional science parks in Thailand, including one in Northern Thailand. The branch at Northern Science Park in Chiang Mai will focus on rice, fruits, vegetables and organic products. In addition, Food Innopolis will work with the science park in Khon

Kaen focused on sugar, rice, and meat and poultry and the science park in Songkla on seafood and Halal food.

Local clusters

The Food Valley and Food Innopolis clusters are overarching initiatives that are inclusive of a number of sub-clusters that operate more locally: the longan cluster (Chiang Mai), functional foods cluster (Chiang Mai), coffee cluster (Chiang Mai), tea cluster (Chiang Rai) and cosmetics cluster (Chiang Mai), etc. Some of these local clusters are very nascent in their development processes and need to be better connected to the broader regional and national innovation systems.

Government financial support programmes for SMEs

Industrial Technology Assistant Programme (ITAP) Grants

ITAP will finance 50% of consulting fees up to a maximum of THB 100 000 per SME for applications for food certification through Good Manufacturing Process, Hazard Analysis Critical Control Point, British Retail Consortium Global Standard for Food Safety, International Standards Organization ISO2200 and Food Safety System Certification FSSC22000 certifications.

It also offers grants to SMEs seeking to purchase an Enterprise Resource Planning (ERP) system to improve their supply chain management. Two programmes are available:

1. 50% of the cost of purchase of an ERP out-of-the-box plus consulting expenses up to a maximum of THB 150 000 per SME.
2. 50% of consulting expenses up to a maximum of THB 300 000 per SME for implementation of a customised ERP system according to company specifications.

ITAP will also finance 50% of R&D expenses up to THB 400 000 for SMEs in the food, medical, automotive, energy and environmental industries with a maximum registered capital of THB 200 million.

The Digital Economy Promotion Agency (DEPA) Voucher

DEPA will finance 50% of the cost up to a maximum of THB 10 000 for a mini-transformation voucher for micro-enterprises, farmers and SMEs. The vouchers can be used to buy software, IT systems and hardware. Some 2 200 vouchers will be available throughout the country on a first-come, first-served basis, with 200 vouchers allocated to the Northern region.

National Innovation Agency (NIA) innovative start-up funding

The NIA aims to promote Thailand as a global start-up investment destination, attracting global venture capital to the region and promoting deep tech start-ups using advanced technology like artificial intelligence in health, food, and agriculture. The NIA's Open Innovation scheme offers grants of up to THB 1.5 million and low interest rate loans to qualifying innovative start-ups. Together with smart visas, the programme aims to help position Thailand as a landing pad for global start-ups (Leesa-Nguansuk, 2019).

Digital Economy Promotion Agency (DEPA) start-up and SME transformation funding

DEPA in collaboration with the United Overseas Bank and the FinLab have established a Smart Business Transformation programme to assist Thai SMEs with technology integration (Boonnoon, 2018). The funds will be split evenly between a Start-up Fund and a DEPA Transformation Fund.

Amounts of THB 50 000, 1 million and 5 million are available through grants, angel funding or co-investment, depending on the size of the project.

National Science and Technology Development Agency (NSTDA) and National Electronics and Computer Technology Centre (NECTEC)

NSTDA and NECTEC provide financial support with a science, technology and digital focus. They operate two programmes for innovative entrepreneurship. The Young Entrepreneurs programme supports university students to create their own businesses and offer vouchers and grants to fund their business to those judged to have successful business plans. The Start-up Voucher Programme is a reimbursement scheme to enable business owners to receive vouchers worth up to THB 800 000 per project to develop a scale-up business (Business Incubation Center, 2018).

Government non-financial support programmes for SMEs

The Department of Business Development (DBD)

The DBD is a government agency under the supervision of the Thai Ministry of Commerce (MOC) with the primary responsibility for regulating and enforcing business legislation including the Foreign Business Act.

DBD holds seminar courses and workshops to educate entrepreneurs. Sample courses include *Starting a Business, Smart Business Solution for SMEs, E-Filing* and *Total Solution for SMEs* (DBD Academy, 2019a).

The DBD's Academy for e-Learning has six curricula and 27 subjects, with a certification process for each subject. Classes are provided free of charge on subjects such as starting a business, finance and accounting, beginner e-commerce and developing strategies for e-commerce (DBD Academy, 2019b).

Department of Intellectual Property

The Department of Intellectual Property provides services such as trademark, copyright and patent registration and protection (Department of Intellectual Property, 2019a). It also offers free seminars and an e-learning site on subjects such as the basics of intellectual property, licensing innovation for commercial use and the power of innovation (Department of Intellectual Property, 2019).

Department of International Trade Promotion (DITP)

The DITP is a government agency that promotes import-export activities through seminars, workshops and trade fairs. It operates an e-Commerce platform www.thaitrade.com to expand trade opportunities for Thai products and companies. It also offers online international trade courses at https://nea.ditp.go.th/. Some examples of its courses are *Startup 101* and *Upgrading Business Processes for International Trading*.

Department of Industrial Promotion (DIP)

The DIP provides a range of consultancy support to industrial businesses. It operates a Business Service Centre (BSC) which offers seminars and provides information to entrepreneurs, individuals and SMEs. It also operates a range of non-financial support programmes to support SME growth (Table 1.5).

Table 1.5. DIP non-financial support for SME development in Thailand

Goal	Strategy
1.	23 Information and Communication Technology Centres (ICTs) provide central machinery, co-working space, consulting and advisory services for SMEs for product development.
2.	The SME Support and Rescue Centre (SSRC) acts as a help desk consultant and assists with problem solving and loan requests. It operates 270 centres serving SMEs at the provincial industrial offices of the DIP.
3.	Training to support SMEs to adjust business models, technology training and business mentoring.
4.	Collection of SME Big Data to analyse SMEs and create access channels to government services.
5.	The Big Brother Guarantee Success Solution connects SMEs with leading national and global companies. Mentor companies include: CP, Betagrow, Thai Union Frozen Foods, Central Grop, Tesco-Lotus, PTT, SCG, Denzo, Delta, Nissan, Honda and Toyota.
6.	Digital Value Chain to link SMEs into a digital B2B platform with Japan. The program is supported by the Japanese Ministry of Economy, Trade and Industry (METI).
7.	Strengthening SME financial literacy, including having a single set of accounts.
8.	Assisting SMEs with meeting standardised certification processes for products and services.
9.	Creative Industry Village. Developing community-based agricultural SME economies with the goal of increasing community income by 25%.

Source: https://www.dip.go.th/th/category/2019-03-24-11-29-11/2019-03-22-10-34-15; http://www.smerescuecenter.com/; https://www.dip.go.th/th/events_details/60y; https://www.dip.go.th/th/events_detail/53364.

Institute for Small and Medium Enterprises Development (ISMED)

ISMED is an institute that provides training seminars and consultancy services for start-ups and SMEs. Examples of its development projects are the Innovation HALAL Cluster Project, SME Regular Level Project and Beyond Beauty ASEAN Bangkok 2019.

The Thai government SME policy response to COVID-19

OECD (2021) summarises the policy measures the Thai government put in place in order to help SMEs to survive the COVID-19 crisis. Measures specifically targeting SMEs include low interest loans, reduction of withholding tax, tax deductions of salary expenses, rapid dissemination of VAT refunds, and rebates on social security payments.

Conclusions and policy recommendations

Many of the conditions that will be required for the development of the advanced agriculture and biotechnology and food-for-the-future sectors in Chiang Mai and Chiang Rai are already in place. They include agricultural production, growing international demand for new healthy functional and medicinal foods, and high-level R&D and knowledge transfer infrastructures. However, there are constraints in developing innovative start-ups and scale-ups to apply R&D results to agricultural production through new products aimed at international markets. This suggests the need for stronger support for start-ups and scale-ups in areas including support for technology adoption, R&D, and access to funding.

It is also important that the government closely monitors the progress of its key policy initiatives aimed at promoting start-ups and scale-ups in the regional innovation cluster. These include notably the Northern Science Park, Food Innopolis, the agri-clusters and business incubators initiatives. There needs to be continuity of support for these programmes and reinforced support where there is positive evaluation evidence of strong impact.

Box 1.3. Recommendations stemming from the regional economic and policy context

- Increase the focus of SME support programmes on existing and potential start-ups and scale-ups with innovation, growth and export potential.
  - Align Key Performance Indications (KPIs) across government organisations with SME growth and innovation objectives.
  - Reduce or eliminate the 'check the box' mentality for approving the participation of SMEs in public support programmes, focusing more on their potential to benefit.
  - Ensure continuity of policies to support start-ups and scale-ups in advanced agriculture and biotechnology and food-for-the-future in Chiang Mai and Chiang Rai and refine the policies based on evaluation evidence.
- Data analytics
  - Create a system to track the success and failure of start-ups, scale-ups and other SMEs that receive public support.
  - Obtain data on different types of SMEs (e.g. new firms, high-growth firms, technology-based firms etc.) covering issues such as number of employees, years in business, type of business, gross/net margins and capital investment. Use this information to guide the design of SME policy and the firms selected to benefit.

References

Arunmas, P. (2019), "Cutting through the gloom in export prospects," 1 July, Bangkok Post, Bangkok, Thailand, https://www.bangkokpost.com/business/1704820/cutting-through-the-gloom-in-export-prospects/.

Asawachintachit, D. (2018), *BOI Policies and Plans for Attracting Investment in 2018*, Board of Investment, Bangkok, Thailand.

https://www.boi.go.th/upload/content/Presentation%20for%20Chambers_final_5a95087c8e170.pdf.

Bangkok Post (2018), "'Narah' Thai herb product wins Gold on the world stage at Hong Kong IIDC 2017," 16 January, *Bangkok Post*, Bangkok, Thailand.

BOI (Board of Investment) (2015), *Thailand Moving Ahead with Cluster Development*, Thailand Board of Investment, Bangkok, Thailand

https://www.boi.go.th/upload/content/BOI-brochure-cluster%20area-EN-20151116_53354.pdf.

BOI (Board of Investment) (2017), *What we do*, Thailand Board of Investment, Bangkok, Thailand,

https://www.boi.go.th/index.php?page=what_we_do2

BOI (2018), *Thailand: Food Industry*, BOI, Bangkok, Thailand, https://www.boi.go.th/upload/content/Food%20industry_5abde0169bf4c.pdf..

Boonnoon, J. (2018), "Bt200m tipped into fund for startups, IT upgrades," 3 May, *The Nation Thailand*, Nation Multimedia Group, Bangkok, Thailand. https://www.nationthailand.com/Economy/30344554/

Business Incubation Center (2018), *Startup Voucher*, NSTDA, Bangkok, Thailand, https://www.nstda.or.th/bic/project.

CMU Corporate Relations and Alumni Center (2018), "Outstanding project, first quarter 2018, CMU Science and Technology Park (STeP)," CMU Corporate Relations and Alumni Center, Chiang Mai,

Thailand.

DBD Academy (2019a), *About DBD Academy*, Department of Business Development, Bangkok, Thailand, http://dbdacademy.dbd.go.th/about/index.

DBD Academy (2019b), *Training / Seminars*, Department of Business Development, Bangkok, Thailand, http://www.dbd.go.th/more_news.php?cid=12.

DIP (2019a), *DIP e-Learning System*, DIP, Bangkok, Thailand, http://elearning.ipthailand.go.th/lms/.

DIP (2019b), "SME Service Center: ITC," 22 March, DIP, Bangkok, Thailand, https://www.dip.go.th/th/category/2019-03-24-11-29-11/2019-03-22-10-34-15

FAOSTAT (2017), Dataset: Crops, Food and Agriculture Organization of the United Nations, Rome, Italy. http://www.fao.org/faostat/en/#data/QC.

Krungthai Bank (2019), "Functional Foods," from *SME Focus June-August 2019*, Krungthai Bank, Bangkok, Thailand.

Leesa-Nguansuk, S. (2019), "*NIA touts startup programme"*, 10 July, Bangkok Post, Bangkok, Thailand. https://www.bangkokpost.com/business/1709743/nia-touts-startup-programme/.

Magnin, C. (2016). *How big data will revolutionize the global food chain*, McKinsey & Company, New York City, USA.

NESDC (National Economic and Social Development Board) (2016), *Thailand 20 Year National Strategy, 2017-2036*, NESDC, Bangkok, Thailand.

NESDC (2019), *Thai Economic Performance in Q1 and Outlook for 2019*, Macroeconomic Strategy and Planning Office, National Economic and Social Development Board, Bangkok, Thailand.

OAE (2019), *Quarterly Report*, Office of Agricultural Economics, Bangkok, Thailand.

Prachachat.net (2019), ธัญญานุภาพ อานันทนะ แม่ทัพ *STeP* มือปั้น *Startup* ดัน ศก.ภาคเหนือโต *2.4* หมื่นล้าน [Tanyanuparb Anantana, Director of STeP, want to grow economy of Northern Thailand by 24 billion baht], https://www.prachachat.net/local-economy/news-297733.

Notes

[1] Advanced agriculture, also referred to as agritech, is a broad term to describe technology that improves agricultural output or the efficiency of "every link in the value chain from field to fork" (Magnin, 2016). This includes every area where technology can impact the supply chain (i.e. optimising production methods, distribution, reducing waste and adapting digital payment systems). Precision farming, robotics, use of satellites or drones for soil and weather mapping and AI are all opportunities in advanced agriculture.

[2] Biotechnology refers to innovations exploiting biological processes for the production of products, including in food science (functional and healthy food), medicine and cosmetics.

[3] The Table below sets out the definitions used to define SMEs in Thailand. Source: Department of Industrial Promotion (DIP), www.dip.go.th.

Sector	Criteria	Micro	Small	Medium
Manufacturing	Employees	1-5	6-50	51-200
	Revenue (million THB)	<1.8	1.8 – 100	100 – 500
Trade and Service	Employees	1-5	6-30	31-100
	Revenue (million THB)	<1.8	1.8 – 50	50 – 300

[4] Information from the Customer Interface Officer at the Chiang Mai University Science and Technology Park (STeP CMU, 2019).

2 The regional entrepreneurial ecosystem

This chapter assesses how policy can improve regional entrepreneurial ecosystem conditions for start-ups and scale-ups in advanced agriculture and biotechnology and food-for-the-future in the Chiang Mai and Chiang Rai regions in Northern Thailand. It assesses the various regional access to resources conditions (connectivity infrastructure, demand for relevant products, business services, talent and skills, access to knowledge, ecosystem leadership and finance) and institutional conditions (regulations, entrepreneurial culture, and networks) for start-ups and scale-ups. The chapter makes policy recommendations to strengthen the regional entrepreneurial ecosystem.

Introduction

The Fourth Thailand SME Promotion Master Plan (2017-2021), prepared by the Office of Small and Medium Enterprise Promotion (OSMEP), sets out the aim: *"to foster the growth of Thai SMEs, enabling them to compete in the international arena, strengthening them to become a major driving force in the country's economy"*. It puts the emphasis on supporting all Thai SMEs to upgrade into smart SMEs, i.e. using appropriate technology to support their activities. The Chiang Mai and Chiang Rai regional innovation cluster can be at the forefront of this development with respect to integrating technology into start-up and scale-up SMEs in advanced agriculture and biotechnology and food-for-the-future.

The generation of innovative start-ups and scale-ups[1] will be critical for the development of the advanced agriculture and biotechnology and food-for-the-future sectors in Chiang Mai and Chiang Rai because these are the firms that will exploit new R&D-based technologies and take them to international markets, hence generating regional income growth. Scale-up enterprises in particular make disproportionate contributions to the creation of new jobs and help build investment confidence in a region and attract inward foreign direct investment (FDI).

In recent years, both innovative start-ups and scale-ups have become an important target for public policy initiatives internationally. These policies seek both to create a favourable business environment in which innovative start-ups and scale-ups can emerge and to target specific potential start-up and scale-up firms and entrepreneurs with support such as advice, finance and networking.

This chapter examines the actions that need to be taken in Thailand to strengthen the Chiang Mai and Chiang Mai regional entrepreneurial ecosystem in advanced agriculture and biotechnology and food-for-the-future, in order to provide an environment in which innovative start-ups and scale-ups are encouraged. It argues that for the long term health of the economy, mechanisms need to be in place for the OSMEP to:

- Identify successfully those start-ups and existing SMEs that are most likely to be innovative and become scale-ups and encourage others to develop the necessary characteristics for such a step.
- Support them through the process by ensuring they have access to knowledge (technical, financial and business development knowledge), mentoring, contacts including international contacts, business acumen, opportunities to share infrastructure, especially technology infrastructure, and finance. Some of this involves the OSMEP acting directly and some through third parties including universities.
- Ensure that successful innovative start-ups and scale-ups help others to follow by taking part in evaluations, information dissemination and future mentoring programmes. This itself feeds into the OSMEP work in seeding and identifying new innovative start-ups and scale-ups.
- Lead this policy area and partner with other organisations to develop complementary activities for innovative start-ups and scale-ups.

There are challenges to overcome. In the Northern Region, there are too many very small firms which are not growing, few medium-sized firms, few technologically-advanced firms and low levels of financial capital. Only 0.47% of firms are classified as medium-sized (50-200 employees with a turnover of THB 500 million),[2] whereas small enterprises account for 99.26% of enterprises. Similarly, only 1.2% of enterprises are in professional, scientific and technical services. Almost all capital is from sources internal to Thailand: 99.9% had no foreign investment or foreign share holdings[3]. There are very few major national and international firms in the key sectors which could act as anchor firms to mentor SMEs into new business models and introduce them into product and service value chains. Low levels of growth capital need to be addressed.

Furthermore, the Fourth Thailand SME Promotion Master Plan notes that Thai SMEs are likely to face increasing competitive pressures resulting from their lack of knowledge and capability in business management, weakness in technological capabilities, and limited capacity to grow and compete internationally. This suggests low levels of absorptive capacity – an organisation's ability to identify, assimilate, transform, and use external knowledge, research and practice (Cohen and Levinthal, 1990).

A further issue is to address low entrepreneurial aspirations in Thailand in the areas of innovative and growth-oriented entrepreneurship.

The sections below review 10 pillars of the Chiang Mai and Chiang Rai regional entrepreneurial ecosystem corresponding to the OECD regional entrepreneurial ecosystem analytical framework. They identify policy issues to address in each pillar. Particular priorities in Chiang Mai and Chiang Rai with respect to innovative start-ups and scale-ups in advanced agriculture and biotechnology and food-for-the-future are:

1. access to finance for scale-ups;
2. talent and skills for entrepreneurship and innovation; and
3. entrepreneurial culture and networks.

The chapter annex offers an overall SWOT analysis of each pillar. The key issues are also outlined in Table 2.1 below.

Table 2.1. Summary of policy issues in the Chiang Mai and Chiang Rai advanced agriculture and food-for-the-future entrepreneurial ecosystem

Ecosystem Pillar	Policy issues	Policy recommendations
Connectivity infrastructure	High logistics costs; low logistics supply chain transparency	Improve digital infrastructure; digital connections by firms; and digital skills training
Demand for relevant products	Untapped opportunities for branding and public procurement	Marketing grants, advice and branding efforts; public procurement initiative for healthcare innovation
Business services	Limited high quality support targeted on scale-ups in existing public business development services schemes	Increase staff capabilities and finance in OSMEP one-stop-shops; increase targeting of advice to scale-ups; channel advice to networks of SMEs
Talent and skills	Student brain drain; few large companies training workers; fragmented public management training programmes; shortages of technical skills	Upgrade university curricula and training quality; support and involve serial entrepreneurs in training
Access to knowledge	Limited university budgets for R&D; low SME absorptive capacity	Develop joint research commercialisation infrastructure across regional universities; support applied research in universities; support universities to provide knowledge to scale-ups; involve retired entrepreneurs as mentors to scale-ups
Ecosystem leadership	National policies lack regional tailoring	Produce a regional entrepreneurship development strategy for Chiang Mai and Chiang Rai
Finance	Little targeting of public financing programmes on high potential start-ups and scale-ups; limited angel and crowdfunding investment	Increase targeting of finance programmes to start-ups and SMEs with scale-up potential; combine finance support with mentoring; develop crowdfunding and business angel initiatives
Regulations	Slow-moving Food and Drug Agency (FDA) license approvals	Provide support to SMEs going through the FDA product license approval process
Entrepreneurial culture	High fear of failure; limited growth-oriented entrepreneurship by women; more potential for academic entrepreneurship; potential for entrepreneurship from returning migrants	Involve entrepreneurs (returning diaspora, university alumni) in awareness raising; provide dedicated entrepreneurship support for women
Networks	Lack of involvement of large firms and universities in firm networks and low trust	Create a networking organisation for the regional innovation cluster

Source: OECD

In developing appropriate policies in these areas, it is essential to adopt a strong focus on start-ups and existing SMEs with the potential to grow, that have scalability (i.e. when their input increases, their output increases faster), and are innovative.

Access to resources conditions

Connectivity infrastructure

To be a player on the national or international scene, firms need to be conveniently connected with collaborators, funders, markets and suppliers. Sometimes physical connectivity is needed but good ICT connectivity can work very well and is sometimes more reliable. For ambitious firms in Chiang Mai and Chiang Rai, physical connectivity to other parts of Thailand's domestic market and international markets is crucial, particularly with ASEAN countries. Connectivity with Bangkok is especially important.

There are two main airports and a number of smaller ones. Chiang Mai International Airport has some 10 million passengers a year, one-fifth of them international. It is a major gateway, with many flights to Bangkok and to China, Singapore and Malaysia. Chiang Rai International Airport is a main domestic gateway airport with frequent Bangkok flights. However there are no direct flights or trains running between Chiang Mai and Chiang Rai. The easiest way to get to Chiang Rai from Chiang Mai is by bus or car taking around three hours. Chiang Mai will benefit from a new rail route linking Chiang Mai to Bang Sue, with onward connectivity to Laos, Cambodia and Malaysia.[4]

ICT connectivity is improving. The "Digital Thailand" initiative aims to transform Thailand through the use of digital technologies in all socioeconomic activities by developing infrastructure, human capital, and other digital resources. There has been progress in putting the digital vision into action, for example through the implementation of "smart city" pilots in Phuket and Chiang Mai and large ICT infrastructure improvements such as extending the coverage of broadband internet to all villages.[5]

Moving physical goods through the supply chain from the North is costly. According to the World Bank Logistics Performance Index, Thailand ranks behind Malaysia and Singapore in overall logistics performance, but ahead of Cambodia, Laos and Myanmar (World Bank, 2018). Logistics costs are currently a limiting factor to importing and exporting. Most raw materials and finished goods are still moved by trucks, which is costly, and there is very little supply chain transparency and very little automation or technology to track processes or identify bottlenecks.

Demand for relevant products

Demand opportunities for scale-ups in advanced agriculture and biotechnology and food-for-the-future are still in the early stages. However, the market for healthy, functional and medicinal foods is expanding as the trend towards healthier living and health-related products grows. The opportunities are being driven by increasing levels of wealth, improved education, targeted government health and wellness campaigns, and globalisation. ASEAN shoppers are increasingly aware of the importance of healthy living, fresh food, nutrition and product sourcing. Another driver will be growing appetites from Chinese consumers for quality agricultural products from Thailand.

The national government is supporting efforts to improve the value chain by focusing on technology and innovation in the following areas:

- Upstream – farming systems, seeding, water, soil and nutrient management, harvesting.
- Midstream – dehydrating, modifying food, packaging, increasing shelf life, food safety.
- Downstream – marketing, distribution.

Branding the regional cluster to distinguish it from other places will enable start-ups and scale-ups to identify with it and use it in their marketing in international markets. A recurrent theme is a lack of a profile of regional success stories.

There is also significant potential to use public procurement in areas related to healthy food to stimulate start-ups and scale-ups in Chiang Mai and Chiang Rai. Box 2.1 gives an example of a scale-up policy in

Canada which aims to scale up companies in health and biosciences by creating a platform for procurement of health innovations by a network of public and private sector health organisations.

Box 2.1. The Canadian CAN Health Network

Description of the approach

The Canadian Health and Biosciences Economic Strategy includes the objective of accelerating innovation adoption through introducing new innovation procurement drawing on the massive scale of health care spending, which reached CAD 253 billion in Canada in 2018 – 11% of the country's GDP. This spending offers many opportunities to procure innovations from start-ups and scale-ups.

In 2020, the Government of Canada announced that it would support a CAD 20 million project proposal to create a network of health care organisations to co-operate on procuring innovations directly from medical technology companies and ensure that the technology is sold into the network, hence stimulating scale-up companies in health and biosciences as well as using innovation to transform products and services.

The CAN Health Network is a national partnership comprised of leading Canadian health organisations, referred to as Edges, and companies across Canada. Edges are a diverse set of public or private organisations with shared challenges that form an integrated network to collaborate, adopt and procure innovative home-grown solutions. Edges may be hospitals, home care organisations, health authorities, private clinics etc. They are health care providers that are committed to being early adopters of innovative Canadian health care solutions. They function as a co-op style placement site working as an integrated marketplace for Canadian businesses to test and enhance their technologies in partnership with the end-user and subsequently scale through innovative procurement processes.

The Network works to introduce new solutions into the health care system, and pave the way for Canadian businesses to scale not only across Canada, but globally. So far the CAN Health Network consists of two regions with 5 provinces; a further four are under development. The Edges identify market-ready needs for the Network and select the best suited companies (which might be mid-to-late stage ventures). They are paired with an Edge, which provides them with multi-level support to ensure optimal product market fit. The companies embed themselves into that Edge for up to a year. A national competitive procurement process is then launched so that all of the Network's members can procure the solution without having to repeat the process.

The Network functions as an integrated market allowing promising companies to work directly with health care organisations to understand their needs and commercialise health technologies and scale up their companies. Through this integrated market, SMEs and leading start-ups work with early-adopter institutions to collaboratively research, develop and refine Canadian medical technologies to make them market-ready. This easy access to a large, consolidated domestic marketplace is designed to provide the opportunity for companies to scale up, commercialising technologies that can be exported around the world, while being anchored in Canada creating jobs.

The network is tackling market access barriers thus enabling Canadian health innovation companies to compete on a national and international level by providing companies with:

- Access to buyers' sites to demonstrate the value of their technology.

- Fast-tracked and scalable procurement utilising existing guidelines.
- An integrated marketplace allowing businesses to scale rapidly.

Success factors

Funding for the establishment of the network has been guaranteed by national government and by two partnerships each worth CAD 3.5 million. This initial investment will build the first points of the national network in Western Canada and Ontario, with further expansion planned for Quebec, Atlantic Canada and Northern Canada. The successes of these initial investments will guide future funding decisions.

The first part of the network in the West of Canada is supported by Western Economic Diversification Canada and led by Saskatchewan Health Authority (SHA). SHA is the largest organisation in Saskatchewan, employing over 40 000 people and physicians responsible for the delivery of high quality and timely health care for the province. SHA leads the Western Network from British Columbia, Alberta, Saskatchewan and Manitoba, with three Edge partners including entire health authorities. SHA is also advising and supporting the creation of the CAN Health Central Network.

It works with:

- Alberta Health Services;
- Children's Hospital Research Institute of Manitoba;
- O'Brien Institute for Public Health, University of Calgary; and
- Vancouver Coastal Health.

In the South East of Canada, CAD 3.5 million will come from FedDev Ontario and Trillium Health Partners and will lead the creation of the CAN Health Network in southern Ontario. It will work with:

- Bruyère;
- Grand River Hospital;
- The Hospital for Sick Children (SickKids);
- Prism Eye Institute;
- SE Health;
- Sinai Health System;
- Sunnybrook Health Sciences Centre;
- University Health Network; and
- Unity Health Toronto.

Challenges

The CAN Health initiative is in its early stages and is yet unproven. However, its aims are consistent with what Hoogenberg (2020) identifies as the main ways forward in scaling up bioscience firms. There is a risk that the model will not be adopted in all the targeted regions, as has been the case with Start-up Canada.

Relevance to Chiang Mai and Chiang Rai

The relevance for the Chiang Mai and Chiang Rai regions lies in the role of national support to create a national network with regional branches that involve regional development agencies, key public sector healthcare organisations and universities. The first two partnerships have been funded by regional-level organisations, so that the networks are focused on specific local knowledge of demand and expertise. The motto for this approach is 'Recognizing Unique Regional Needs and Opportunities Under One National Network'.

In Chiang Mai and Chiang Rai, health organisations could work together with potential scale-up firms on Northern Science Park in the areas of biotech and healthy foods, targeted for example at ageing populations, with the involvement of the universities and the Thailand Centre of Excellence for Life Sciences (TCELS). The OSMEP would have a key role to play in providing overall leadership of the initiative.

Sources of further information:
"Government of Canada Commits $20 Million To Scale Up Health & Bioscience Companies", July 2019 https://www.biomb.ca/news/567/government-of-canada-commits-20-million-to-scale-up-health-bioscience-companies
https://canhealthnetwork.ca/
Hoogenberg, D. (2020), "How biotech scale ups can contribute to the health industry transformation", EY Netherlands, Rotterdam, https://www.ey.com/en_nl/health/how-biotech-scale-ups-can-contribute-to-the-health-industry-transformation

Business services

Business development services suppliers provide advice, consultancy, management training and mentoring to scale-ups to help them improve their management practices and technologies and to develop entrepreneurial capacity.

Private business services suppliers are service minded, but costs are still high for SMEs. Therefore there is substantial reliance by SMEs on national public business development services programmes. For example, the OSMEP One-Stop Service is present in every province. It offers SMEs support with accessing researchers and experts, testing and analysis, standards and regulation, equipment and machinery and incentives to work with new technology so that they can scale up. However, these programmes provide largely basic support to large numbers of firms, and there is potential to offer public support to private providers to supply higher-quality, more specialised business development services to firms with scale-up potential.

The aim should be to upgrade SMEs through critical points in their development (e.g. start up, scale up, first export, new product). Product and market training services could include value chain competitive analysis, upgrading use of technology (especially digital technology), market analysis, business canvas models[6], and managing risk and partnerships. Capacity building support should also be provided in intellectual property (IP) and IP protection.

Groups of innovative start-ups and potential scale-ups in advanced agriculture and biotechnology and food-for-the-future could also be supported with business development services to upgrade their business models at the same time as integrating R&D in their products. SMEs should be selected for more intensive business development support on the basis of their absorptive capacity although all SMEs need help in scanning for business opportunities, short to long term.

Common programmes and collective action between business support agencies are also required. This would be helped by the creation of an entrepreneurship hub through which business services and mentoring would be delivered to groups of SMEs.

A further consistent message from regional stakeholders in the provision of business services in the Northern region is that local intervention is needed in training the trainers who then mentor SMEs.

Talent and skills

Talented entrepreneurs

Scale-up entrepreneurship is favoured by the presence of highly-skilled entrepreneurs in a region. In advanced agriculture and biotechnology and food-for-the-future a key potential source of scale-up entrepreneurs is Science, Technology, Engineering and Maths (STEM) graduates from regional universities. However, a challenge is that many STEM graduates from Chiang Mai and Chiang Rai universities are attracted out of the region to work in large employers (like CP, Betagrow, Central Foods, Thai Union Frozen Foods and Thai-Bev) in Bangkok and other regions, which generally offer higher salaries and more diverse opportunities. This may discourage graduates from setting up their own firms. There are also few large enterprises in Chiang Mai and Chiang Rai where employees can receive training and experience in business and management that could help them in subsequently creating their own enterprises.

Potential innovative start-up and scale-up entrepreneurs can also be mentored locally or attracted from other regions and countries. There are government programmes in Thailand that support this, including Career for the Future Academy (run by NSDTA) for mentors and entrepreneurs; and the Smart Visa programme (run by BOI with NIA and DEPA) designed to attract highly-skilled workers, investors, executives and start-up entrepreneurs wishing to work or invest in targeted STEM industries in Thailand.

Serial entrepreneurs have been found to be an important driver of cluster development in many OECD countries. For example in Cambridge, United Kingdom, they have created many spin-out enterprises from the University and other companies (Beveridge, 2001). There is very little evidence of serial entrepreneurship in Chiang Mai and Chiang Rai as yet, but the Northern Science Park has created a fund to reinvest in entrepreneurs to "serialise" them. This would build on the expertise of alumni and develop them as mentors, as is the case in the Little Onion Factory (https://www.littleonionfactory.com/).

Management skills in SMEs

Training and mentoring needs to be more available for upskilling SME managers in firms with scale-up potential, for example in the areas of management, marketing and exporting. Mentoring could be organised into groups of SMEs with scale-up potential, enabling co-learning and increasing networking. In the past, management training programmes have been fragmented across agencies and short term. A better approach would be to create a platform management programme with different streams according to SME sector and size of firm and deliver a longer-term programme in co-operation across different government agencies.

Universities, especially Business Schools, should also be more involved in building management skills in industry. Their faculty could provide mentoring and consultancy to start-ups and scale-ups. They could also be involved in introducing continuous professional development for managers and technical staff, as is common in the UK for example.[7]

Workforce skills

In general, there are shortages of skilled workers in agritech and biotechnology in Chiang Mai and Chiang Rai. Most of the relevant technical education is geared towards food sciences (Chong, 2019). A greater emphasis on STEM education as well as critical thinking and decision making skills would complement this and help fill shortages of a range of skills needed for a growing technology company – qualified software engineers, coders, technicians and research scientists etc.

Universities could help ensure that alumni have relevant business skills through developing joint scientific and engineering degree programmes with business schools, involving industry practitioners as well as scientists. An example is the MSc in BioBusiness at Birkbeck, University of London.[8] This approach would be consistent with the National Biotechnology Policy Framework 2012-2021 in which the Thai government called for human resource development programmes to increase the number of graduates in the field of modern biological science.[9] Joint programmes could be developed with international advanced agriculture firms.

Universities could also collectively adopt new models of teaching and new targets to address start-up and scale-up needs, e.g. through advanced apprenticeship programmes, internships, Masters dissertations on industry-relevant problems, or a classroom in a scale-up factory. The latter approach is illustrated by the Faculty on the Shopfloor as delivered by Coventry University in the United Kingdom (Box 2.2).

Box 2.2. Faculty on the Shop Floor, Coventry University, United Kingdom

Description of the approach

Successful technology transfer models in leading-edge technologies all include an essential element of training/staff development in target firms. The collaboration between Coventry University and Unipart Manufacturing Group (UMG) in developing the Institute for Advanced Manufacturing and Engineering (AME), known as the "faculty on the factory floor" illustrates a model for achieving this.

AME was established at Unipart Manufacturing, a car components company in Coventry in the West Midlands region. Its three elements are (i) teaching and skills, (ii) engagement with business and (iii) commercialising R&D. It took its first cohort of students in September 2014.

The region as a whole suffers from skill shortages, with major employers recruiting from a limited pool. To overcome this, the Coventry and Warwickshire Local Enterprise Partnership (LEP) set an initial target of training 5 000 new or unskilled engineers by 2015. It also aimed to increase the number of local SMEs active in R&D. To engage with this agenda, Coventry University and Unipart agreed to build a partnership that incorporated joint R&D activity and training activity, supported by the new AME facility.

Central Government funding of GBP 1 million was allocated to the project from the Local Growth Fund by a competitive process following a bid by the Coventry and Warwickshire Local Enterprise Partnership (CWLEP), which represents local businesses, universities, colleges and local government authorities. Coventry University provided a further GBP 4 million to refurbish the additional building to equip it with state-of-the-art digital manufacturing and materials analysis equipment, and received part funding from the Catalyst Fund of the Higher Education Funding Council for England (HEFCE, which has since been replaced by Innovate UK). Unipart contributes GBP 17.9 million per year towards the partnership and a further GBP 6.5 million towards student scholarships and product research and investment.

Around 100 students study at the site. Since AME was launched, all students who have graduated have been employed in engineering jobs. Selected students receive scholarships of GBP 3 000 and access to summer placements from Unipart. Students can also access career development opportunities after graduation including management training, internships, international placement, and employment opportunities across the Unipart Group and with other leading manufacturers. AME also offers fully funded PhD studentships.

Factors for success

The success of the partnership is that it is embedded in each organisation's strategy and involves teachers, trainers and researchers from both organisations working together alongside students. Coventry University benefits from access to up-to-date equipment and practical knowledge. Its 'activity-led learning' model underpins teaching, prioritising practical, work-based learning for students. Industrial advisory boards are active in curriculum design to ensure that programmes remain up to date and relevant. The new building and manufacturing equipment has been designed to provide learning spaces and resources.

One key to success is strong leadership from both organisations' senior teams. Another is shared fundamental principles such as a focus on skills development in a workplace environment. Others include close collaboration on applied research, co-location to foster communication, and a desire to align both partners' measures of success. The project would not succeed without senior level engagement, the co-location of staff, and joint appointments.

All of this has fostered the collaboration and the culture change required to work together effectively and speed up decision-making.

External support from the Local Enterprise Partnership (i.e. CWLEP) and the HEFCE Catalyst Fund has also been important. This gave Unipart and Coventry University sufficient confidence to release their own funds to support the initiative. Accreditation from relevant professional bodies (Institution of Engineering and Technology and the Institution of Mechanical Engineers) enhanced its reputation among potential students (particularly from outside the United Kingdom) and with employers. AME's facilities and expertise – as a University research centre – have already been used to secure funding for low-carbon technology research projects focused on aerospace, automotive, rail, oil and gas, and power generation. It has received funding for six research projects worth over GBP 2.5 million.

Obstacles encountered and responses

Early obstacles included getting all the partners to sign up and apply for funding, finding suitable buildings, marketing the degree and making it inclusive in order to attract more women students. Developing new industry-focused and globally-relevant programmes involving considerable employer input also took time. In addition, new working practices created to fit the new "Faculty on the Factory Floor" approach have required time to bed in. Essentially, an initial "culture clash" has been overcome.

Relevance for Chiang Mai and Chiang Rai regions

While AME is in the field of advanced manufacturing rather than biotechnology, the fundamental principles of an offsite facility of a university hosted by a local employer for jointly-designed R&D and training are transferable. The strength of the approach is that it brings together skill sets in the science base, both students and faculty, with those in industry, to give more relevant training and R&D. Teaching by both university and companies leads to a very fast assimilation of new ideas and practices by the students, as well as learning experiences and improved student employability for the university and knowledge transfers and a source of new employees for the participating firm.

The model could be adapted to a group of SMEs in the advanced agriculture and biotechnology and food-for-the-future sectors that could collaborate with a university on projects that are adapted to the specific needs of different firms in the sectors. The national government would need to provide core funding and the universities would need to allocate resources, but these could be 'in-kind' in the form of time of the lecturing staff. The involvement of local firms is also necessary for analysing skills needs and developing appropriate training.

Source: OECD (2019) Local Entrepreneurship Ecosystems and Emerging Industries: Case Study of Coventry and Warwickshire, United Kingdom.

Universities in Thailand often have a problem in teaching the latest skills because of out-of-date teaching materials, kit and methods. Academic staff could be encouraged to apply for study leave to update their knowledge and practice abroad. This would be on an 'education for return' basis as is practised in Malta's university where agreement to go often involves a contractual commitment to return for a period of time. Involving industry in syllabus development also leads to more up-to-date curricula.

Industry mobility schemes can also play a role in upgrading skills in SMEs. Existing public programmes in Thailand include Talent Mobility (operated by ONES), which relocates personnel temporarily from universities and public research institutions to the private sector to increase business competencies in innovation, and Work Integrated Learning (operated by ONES), a programme for producing vocational and undergraduate level workers for particular STEM sectors. In addition, students could undertake 'on the job' technology transfer to SMEs.

Access to knowledge

Start-ups and scale-ups need to be able to access the latest R&D relevant to their own product and service development in order to take innovations to market. The regional universities and science parks play a key role in injecting technologies into firms in advanced agriculture and biotechnology and food-for-the-future in Chiang Mai and Chiang Rai. However a key barrier is the absorptive capacities of existing SMEs.

Universities

A major strength of Chiang Mai and Chiang Rai is the knowledge resources and services that their universities are providing in advanced agriculture and biotechnology and food-for-the-future and their recent engagement with start-ups and scale-ups.

Table 2.2 lists universities and faculties with relevant specialist expertise and gives examples of their industry engagement practice.

Table 2.2. University support for start-ups and scale-ups in advanced agriculture and biotechnology and food-for-the-future in Chiang Mai and Chiang Rai

University and Department/Centre	Support for start-ups and scale-ups
Chiang Mai University (www.cmu.ac.th) (located in Chiang Mai province) Public research university with strong emphasis on engineering, science, agriculture, and medicine. 39 000 students (10 000 masters students)	
Faculty of Pharmacy https://www.pharmacy.cmu.ac.th/eng2016/index.php	• Provides graduates to pharmaceutical sectors and aims to develop and disseminate advanced pharmaceutical knowledge that benefits society.
Faculty of Agro Industry	• Co-operates with government and private business clusters. • Provides access to the alumni association. • Works with art, cultural and religious organisations and local communities. • Provides seminars, agricultural training, packaging and design. • Provides continuing education to the local community.
Agricultural Technology Service Center (http://www.agri.cmu.ac.th)	• Provides education and training in agriculture. • 19 seminars and workshops in 2018. • Workshops for SMEs, including start-ups, in 2018. • Operates central testing laboratory. • Soil testing. • Plant tissue testing. • Animal feed testing. • Conducts agricultural clinics on best practices for farm, fertilizer and pesticide management.
Food Innovation and Packaging Centre (FIN) (www.fin.cmu.ac.th)	• Supports product development and packaging design. • Provides testing services. • Conducts food innovation policy and R&D support. • Conducts food collaborative research and business development. • Serves as a business incubator.
Science and Technology Park (STeP) – (www. step.cmu.ac.th)	• Provides support on technology and innovation, agriculture, food, medical and biotechnology. • Provides IT software, digital content, IoT, energy technology and materials support. • Supports SMEs and start-up development. • Connects universities with the private sector.

Mae Jo University Business Incubator (MJUBI) (www.mjubi.mju.ac.th)	• Provides business education to the university community consisting of faculty members, researchers, students, alumni and small business owners. • Provides consulting services to entrepreneurs in business processes, innovation, production, marketing, management and accounting. • Conducts research collaboration, proof of technology, technology development and commercialisation. • Manages and maintains intellectual property belonging to the university (https://erp.mju.ac.th/researchDetailPublicEN.aspx?rid=6168).
Mae Fah Luang University https://en.mfu.ac.th (located in Chiang Rai province) Public university with a strong emphasis on science, cosmetics, tea and coffee production and agriculture	
School of Science	• Works with cosmetics companies – uses knowledge in business research for SMEs to connect to the university. • Works with 3 to 4 SMEs to improve products and processing and enhancing products.
School of Agro-industry http://agro-industry.mfu.ac.th/en	• Teaching and research in food technology and technology management of agricultural produce and packaging. • Graduates competent agro-industry technologists for industry and offers continuing professional development. • Helps SMEs with packaging and how to develop products.
Health Science	• Works with herb companies, helping them to develop technology, recruit and export.
Tea Coffee Institute http://web2.mfu.ac.th	• Provides a knowledge and technology transfer centre for tea and coffee products. • Serves as a centre of educational, research and development on tea. • Works as a collaboration and network centre for tea research in both the domestic and international markets. • Implement policies to improve quality and additional tea and coffee. • Provides services including technical research and clinical trials for entrepreneurs
Center of Excellence in Natural Product Innovation	• Provides lab testing services for cosmetic ingredients, and conducts research and development on natural products.
School of Management	• Helps companies in coffee industry.
Mae Fah Luang University Business Incubator (MFUBI) (http://mfubi.mfu.ac.th)	• Works with SME start-ups in the agriculture, health and cosmetic sectors.
Mae Fah Luang Intellectual Property Management and Innovation Department Office http://mfii.mfu.ac.th	• Serves as a centre for technology commercialisation and provides innovation design and IP to the private sector. • Looks after IP rights and patents, undertakes IP asset management for operators and professors in the university • Channels research results to the private sector. • It can refer SMEs to other universities or agencies for example in Bangkok. • Has filed 5 patents for SMEs and drafted more than 100 for faculty.
Chiang Rai Rajabhat University (located in Chiang Rai province) http://www.crru.ac.th/2019/ Public Higher Education Institute	
Faculty of Science and technology http://science.crru.ac.th/	• Food Science Programme • Biological Sciences Programme • Agricultural Technology Programme

Faculty of Management Science http://research.crru.ac.th/rdiwebsite/	• Local industry co-operation on business development and management skills
Rajamangala University of Technology Lanna (includes a campus in Chiang Mai province and a campus in Chiang Rai province) https://www.rmutl.ac.th/ A technology and vocational learning university with campuses across Thailand.	
Faculty of Sciences and agricultural technology https://sat.rmutl.ac.th/	• Local industry co-operation e.g. co-operation with Siriraj-TCELS and network partners on research and development of an innovative nano dust-mite cloth mask with COVID-19 protection

Source: OECD interviews with regional university stakeholders, 2019.

A major asset and potential anchor for the regional entrepreneurial ecosystem is Chiang Mai University, which was designated as the first provincial university in Thailand. Its mission is to establish innovation in the region including through relevant R&D and generating appropriately skilled labour for industry development. The University has some 2 200 researchers.

In Chiang Rai, a key player is Mae Fah Luang University. Its tea and coffee institute provides specialist expertise to local firms and supports them to improve the standard of their products. The University has its own fund for researchers, which can be used for collaborations with regional start-ups and scale-ups, helps SMEs with IP issues, and helps firms apply for Ministry of Industry funding.

Rajabat University and Rajamangala University of Technology Lanna have somewhat different missions. Rajabat University trains teachers and has a budget from the government to leverage the University's skills for local community development. It has no specific budget for SME development, but holds start-up competitions and organises seminars for start-up entrepreneurs. Rajamangala University of Technology Lanna is a vocational training university and organises a range of training and development activities with local industry.

However, the full potential driving role of these universities for the development of advanced agriculture and biotechnology and food-for-the-future in the regions is constrained by limited budgets to develop R&D that can be translated into commercial opportunities for SMEs in key industries for their regions. For example, although receiving government support, Chiang Mai University has to find matching funding for every project. It does this by submitting proposals to different ministries and to the Chiang Mai provincial government budget. Around half of the budget is from ONES.

In a promising development, Chiang Mai University has recently created a licensing holding company. This enables it to gain revenue by licensing technology to existing companies or tech start-ups. This should increase knowledge transfer to start-ups and scale-ups in a familiar model in advanced economies.

Science Parks

The Northern Science Park (NSP), established in 2012, is based at Chiang Mai University and is the bridge between university and industry. The responsible agency is the Science Park Promotion Agency. The NSP works on an open innovation concept, bringing in businesses to participate in R&D work as needed and seeking commercialisation opportunities. Its objectives include developing successful start-ups and scale-ups and providing opportunities to access venture capital.

The NSP works on a three-stage process from start-up through to scale-up: pre-incubation (3-6 months), incubation (up to 3 years) and acceleration (depends on company). It operates three models:

- 'Inside Out'. This involves licensing to an industry translational research fund to take research to proof of concept stage, and then to upscale the research, including IP protection.
- 'Outside In'. What industry wants. This means finding appropriate experts in the university (working with 45 members of staff) and offering appropriate consultancy and research inputs.
- 'Start-up Approach'. Start-up from research. This involves several sectors, students, alumni and academics.

The NSP has generated some 150 start-ups from 7 universities including approximately 50 in Chiang Mai. Some 17% are in medical and biotechnology, one-half are in agriculture, one-quarter in IT software and digital content, and 10% in energy. However, the largest of these start-ups had only 15 employees in 2019, so the NSP is some way from creating substantial scale-up activity. Most companies are at early stages of development with nearly half getting seed-corn funding and a small percentage waiting for fund-raising (5%). Exit is usually through acquisition.

The NSP might also encourage more commercialisation of R&D to start-ups and scale-ups in the regions by hosting NSTDA events in the field of advanced agriculture and biotechnology and food-for-the-future in the Northern Region. These events are designed to bring technology nearing market to potential SME customers, such as the Tech Shows held in Bangkok[1].

The absorptive capacities of SMEs

Knowledge exchange from universities, research laboratories and science parks to start-ups and scale-ups in the regional cluster faces a substantial barrier in the low capacity of SMEs to absorb and apply the relevant technology developed by the universities and the NSP. This gap between university and industry is known locally as the Valley of Challenge. For example, a recent Global Entrepreneurship Monitor (GEM) National Expert Survey of Thailand (Guelich, 2018) reported that lack of R&D transfer from research institutions, universities and/or government agencies to enterprises is considered a major constraint by experts in Thailand. A number of aspects to this barrier lie in limited SME absorptive capacities.

Financing is an important aspect of the problem. Although there are some funding measures, such as the IRTC, which provides matching funding at 50% to develop R&D-based products in start-ups and scale-ups, there is a general lack of support for growth finance.

Also missing is a realisation by start-ups and scale-ups of the need to assert and protect intellectual property (IP). This is crucial for SMEs to take full advantage of innovations.

Lack of skills and networks can also be an issue. More could be done in Chiang Mai and Chiang Rai to transfer technology from universities to start-ups by involving a student who works with a researcher on the commercialisation. A mentoring programme can also play a role. There are a number of foreign mentors in Chiang Mai and Chiang Rai, often brought in by venture capital firms, who come for a number of days because they can see the high potential of an SME. Mentors also come to the regions from Bangkok. However, Thailand lacks a strong body of retired people working as mentors, which by contrast is very important in innovation clusters in other countries, including in Silicon Valley, United States.

Ecosystem leadership

Ecosystem leadership is about developing a vision and strategy for entrepreneurship and innovation that key local stakeholders support. It implies a system for identifying and addressing obstacles to the development of the advanced agriculture and biotechnology and food-for-the-future industries in Chiang Mai and Chiang Rai working across stakeholders. In some regional entrepreneurial ecosystems this leadership role is taken by prominent successful entrepreneurs, businesses, HEIs, or cluster management organisations. However, ecosystem leadership can also be driven by government actors working at the regional level in a way that brings together local stakeholders to assess how to respond to local issues.

The BOI, DIP and the OSMEP are key government departments and bodies leading policy support for SMEs and start-ups nationally. However, they work largely with a national lens and do not focus strongly on identifying and responding to regional bottlenecks affecting entrepreneurship development in particular driving sectors for future growth of the Thai economy, such as advanced agriculture and biotechnology and food-for-the-future in Chiang Mai and Chiang Rai.

Provincial government could potentially work in collaboration with the national government organisations to help with tailoring of SME and entrepreneurship policies to regional needs. However, the provincial level of government has currently not made strong impacts on regionalising the nature of SME and entrepreneurship support.

Another option for generating the necessary regional entrepreneurial ecosystem leadership is the creation of a cluster management organisation for advanced agriculture and biotechnology and food-for-the-future in Chiang Mai and Chiang Rai. This could work with national and regional government ministries and agencies, HEIs, research laboratories such as NSTDA, science parks, and private firms and their representative organisations, including the Federation of Thai Industries and Chambers of Commerce. It would identify regional bottlenecks in the development of the advanced agriculture and biotechnology and food-for-the-future sectors and develop tailored and co-ordinated solutions. The OSMEP could take a leadership role in setting up this organisation and providing basic operational resources.

A shared policy strategy needs to be developed involving all these stakeholders and setting out the respective roles of the different public ministries and agencies. It could be modelled on regional strategies profiled by the European Entrepreneurial Regions project,[2] which identifies and rewards European Union regions developing an outstanding and innovative entrepreneurial policy strategy. As well as identifying the issues that policy needs to address and prioritising the policy interventions in areas such as business advice, finance and skills, developing a regional entrepreneurial ecosystem development strategy for Chiang Mai and Chiang Rai (potentially focused on the advanced agriculture and biotechnology and food-for-the-future cluster) would help address other policy challenges affecting the regions, such as increasing coherence across the interventions of different public bodies, making programmes more sustainable over time, and improving policy performance by setting goals and measuring outcomes.

Finance

Finance is a key area where start-ups and scale-ups need support. Very small firms do not have spare capacity for innovation and growth unless funded. Access to bank loans is important, but access to equity finance and a range of alternative financing instruments such as business angel investment and crowdfunding are also vital aspects of a healthy regional entrepreneurial ecosystem.

In terms of access to bank loans, there are a number of obstacles for start-ups and scale-ups in Chiang Mai and Chiang Rai. Based on a Bank of Thailand study, as many as 5.2 million SMEs received loans from Thai commercial banks in 2017. However, the DIP has identified the following significant barriers to accessing bank financing, which are often likely to be particularly important for potential scale-up enterprises:

- Lack of historical records and information at financial institutions.
- Complexity and difficulty of the application procedures.
- Lack of loan collateral.
- High up-front costs (e.g. 3% of desired credit line).
- Inflexible credit plans and facilities.
- Failure of banks to regularly review SME performance.
- Lack of alignment between the key performance indicators (KPIs) of banks and SME pain points.
- Lack of competition among banks for SME business and lack of diversity of financing offers.
- Aggressive pursuit of businesses that do not require capital by banks.

Venture capital is available, including through the firms listed in Table 2.3, and the government has introduced tax privileges for investors to boost supply, such as income tax exemptions for incomes from investments. However, venture capital is generally in short supply in Thailand. Domestic investments could be complemented by foreign venture capital. However, foreign venture capital firms often have difficulty finding suitable businesses in Thailand due to the restrictions of the Foreign Business Act and the fact that larger deals are constrained by the limited numbers of SMEs in Thailand with an Asian region or multi-national focus. Thailand's banking regulations are not conducive to conducting international business. The inability to trade in U.S. dollars or hold foreign currency and the high cost of letters of credit are also significant obstacles for SMEs.

Table 2.3. Sample of local venture capital firms in Thailand

1.	Beacon Venture Capital (Kasikorn Bank)
2.	N-Vest Venture
3.	Vnet Capital Co., Ltd.
4.	Lombard Investments
5.	InVent (Intouch Holdings PLC)
6.	Bangkok Venture Club (Angel Investment Group)
7.	Finansa PLC
8.	Siri Venture (Siam Commercial Bank)
9.	TukTuk500 Fund

Source: OECD interviews with regional finance stakeholders

The Market for Alternative Investment is a stock exchange for smaller firms in Thailand. SMEs can raise capital there if they have over THB 1 million in paid-up capital after IPO. It provides a platform to raise capital at a lower paid-up level than in the stock exchange of Thailand. In 2016, there were 134 listed companies with a market capitalisation of THB 425 billion. Of these, the only company from the advanced agriculture and biotechnology and food-for-the-future sectors in Chiang Mai and Chiang Rai was Sunsweet in Chiang Mai. The other companies listed were mainly health service firms or property and construction firms. There were none in Chiang Rai.

There is an array of government support programmes that help start-ups and scale-ups to access finance for their development. Current national schemes which are relevant in providing funding to support start-ups and scale-ups advanced agriculture and biotechnology and food-for-the-future in Chiang Mai and Chiang Rai are:

- **Start-up Voucher** (operated by the NSDTA). This supports market expansion for tech start-ups. It offers up to THB 800 000 covering up to 75% of eligible expenses for a market study and consultancy fees from a marketing expert to access foreign and domestic markets. The voucher appears to be effective. However, the focus should be on developing technologies needed in the future. Quality control and feedback also need more consideration.
- **Innovation Vouchers** (operated by the NIA).
- **Technology and innovation-based Enterprise Development Fund** (operated by the MHES). This offers a matching grant or 'conditional recoverable' grant for the development of new products or services or new production/service processes. Target groups are university or vocational education students or students who graduated not over 7 years ago, university or research institution personnel, SMEs, and start-ups which affiliate with universities or research institutions.
- **Competitiveness Fund Programme** (operated by the BOI). This is a new finance programme for private sector companies in 10 target industries.
- **Research Gap Fund** (operated by the NSTDA).
- **R&D and innovation tax incentives** (operated by the NSDTA). All private sector companies are eligible for a tax incentive of between 200% and 300% of R&D and innovation (R&D&I) expenditures up to a project value of THB 3 million. Eligible costs include R&D, training, automation and equipment, IP and technology acquisition, design and IP registration.

- **Credit guarantees** (operated by the Thai Credit Guarantee Corporation – TGC). This is a state-owned specialised financial institution. This aims to ensure that viable SMEs with good credit and at least three years of operational experience have access to bank loans and are not constrained by their lack of capital. A scheme could also be developed to permit SMEs to use IP as collateral. The TCG typically charges SMEs 1.0-2.0% annually based on their annual credit limit.
- **Corporate Income Tax exemption** (operated by the Ministry of Finance). Under this programme, start-ups can receive corporate income tax exemptions when they obtain venture capital and business angel investments.
- **Innovation and Technology Assistance Programme (ITAP)** (operated by the NSDTA). This comprises 18 networks that provide finance for innovation and consultancy. Three of the networks are in the North, accounting for some 13% of ITAP-supported projects in food and agriculture. A new programme ITAP Innovation-Driven Entrepreneurship is being launched for SMEs taking research from lab stage into commercialisation stage with a focus on business growth. However, a bottleneck lies in an insufficient budget for a blanket approach that would enable the programme to cover all SMEs coming forward for support and the problem of lacking a mechanism in current conditions that could channel support only to suitable SMEs that have absorptive capacity.
- **SMEs Private Equity Trust Fund** (operated by the Government Savings Bank). This Fund is worth THB 2 billion for private equity investments in start-ups, scale-ups and SMEs.
- **Venture Capital Fund** (operated by the OSMEP). This is a public venture capital fund that invests in innovative SMEs. The scale of investment has currently been limited, reflecting difficulties in identifying appropriate targets. In the Venture Capital for SME-OTOP programme, government banks provide another source of capital for SMEs through joint investment.
- **The Small and Medium Enterprise Development Bank of Thailand** (SMED Bank) is a state-owned bank that supports SMEs through venture capital funding and business consulting workshops.

However, there is as yet little explicit targeting of the schemes above on those start-ups and scale-ups with the most potential for innovation-based growth in the sectors with potential to drive future Thai economic growth, including high potential firms in advanced agriculture and biotechnology and food-for-the-future in Chiang Mai and Chiang Rai. It is concerning that there are several examples of export-orientated SMEs from Chiang Mai and Chiang Rai (i.e. some of the firms with the highest aspirations) moving to Singapore in order to obtain risk-willing capital. A further obstacle is that there is not enough complementary consultancy, advice, mentoring and other support provided to start-ups and scale-ups alongside the financing.

Furthermore, business angel finance is essential. As Politis (2008) demonstrates, business angels perform a number of important support roles for the businesses they invest in alongside finance, by including business mentoring, network development and due diligence in their interactions. While smart money exists in Thailand, what is desperately short is the kind of finance which brings mentoring into the financing process. Where the Northern region is particular weak is in angel investors. For example, no investments are listed in Chiang Mai and Chiang Rai in the Thailand Startups organisation list of angel investors.[3]

There is scope for local policy makers to work with local business people and financial organisations to develop a community of business angels with a specific focus on advanced agriculture and biotechnology and food-for-the-future. A model could be the London's Angels programme in MedCity, which brings potential investors together with life sciences experts. It is aimed both at people who are experienced investors as well as people who have little or no experience in the life sciences sector http://www.angelsinmedcity.org.uk/.

Crowdfunding is supervised by the Securities and Exchange Commission but needs to be expanded and much better targeted to smart SMEs and scale-ups. An initiative could be taken to stimulate the creation of a crowdfunding platform for innovative SMEs with a Northern regional focus.

Institutional conditions

Regulations

Two major local regulatory conditions, one enabling and one a bottleneck, dominate for innovative start-ups and scale-ups in advanced agriculture and biotechnology and food-for-the-future in Chiang Mai and Chiang Rai. The enabler is the creation of a cluster-based special economic zone (SEZ), Food Innopolis, providing tax incentives to innovative food enterprises located at the NSP at Chiang Mai University, as well as in various other locations in the country. Through the SEZ, investment projects in specific food-related industries are exempt from corporate income tax for five to ten years with a 50% reduction in tax for a further five years (or an additional two years of exemption). In addition, the projects have access to further key national programmes and incentives. Eligible investments can include R&D and scientific testing activities.

The bottleneck is the slow-moving registration process involved in gaining Thai Ministry of Public Health, Food and Drug Administration (FDA) approval for new innovative products. Backlogs occur in the process to obtain licenses for moderate- to high-risk medical devices, novel foods, food supplements, and innovative herbal products. Stakeholders report that the FDA lacks sufficient qualified officers to examine technical dossiers to assess the quality, efficacy, and safety of products. As many of the start-ups and scale-ups in advanced agriculture and biotechnology and food-for-the-future in Chiang Mai and Chiang Rai are innovating through developing health-related products, they need FDA approval before they can market. However, the process is not timely. To get around the problem, many Thai SMEs now seek approval through the Singapore FDA in order to sell products domestically and internationally, which also gives wider credibility and branding. The problem is being addressed nationally but further support could also be offered locally, for example by business development services consultants, to support SMEs through the process without unnecessary delays.

Entrepreneurial culture

Attitudes to entrepreneurship are very positive in Thailand, particularly in the North of Thailand. According to the Global Entrepreneurship Monitor (GEM), some 74% of male adults in the North of Thailand perceived entrepreneurial opportunities in 2018, which is the highest rate in the country. The percentage of women in the North who view entrepreneurship as a desirable career choice was also the highest in the country at 81% (Guelich, 2018). On the other hand, Thais have a high fear of failing compared to other ASEAN countries, 64% for females and 56% for males (Guelich, 2018). This may explain why many Thai entrepreneurs are reluctant to be a 'first mover' and may also contribute to a 'copy culture', whereby entrepreneurs are more comfortable starting a business based on an existing model.

There is particular potential to stimulate more growth-oriented entrepreneurship among women in Chiang Mai and Chiang Rai. The GEM survey indicates that in 2018, women entrepreneurs accounted for 32% of start-up entrepreneurs in Bangkok, but only 11% in the North. Furthermore, female entrepreneurs were less likely than men to expect to grow their companies and much more likely to be fearful of failure (69%), perhaps because they are "entrepreneurs of necessity" (Guelich, 2018). In seeking to support an entrepreneurial culture, there is a need to recognise gender differences and provide appropriate support for women entrepreneurs.

There are many initiatives offered by banks and entrepreneurs to help build an entrepreneurial culture by offering networking and funding to help entrepreneurs to grow their businesses. Examples include NEXT Real by Land & Houses, Kaisikorn Bank's S100 and Everest programmes, SME Transformation, and Siam Commercial Bank's (SCB) Innovative Entrepreneur Programme and Young Entrepreneur Programme. Participants pay high fees to attend but are given access to very successful business people and entrepreneurs. These tools help to promote entrepreneurship and develop positive role models.

Two networks of entrepreneurs are present in Chiang Mai and Chiang Rai, one local and one national. The local one is key for the development of the regional innovation cluster: Chiang Mai Entrepreneurship Association was founded by Thai and international entrepreneurs in Chiang Mai to "connect entrepreneurs, build an ecosystem and develop local talent." This network could be further supported at the regional level, for example by hosting joint network events and developing a regional profile for successful entrepreneurs in the Association.[4] This would further help build the local entrepreneurial culture.

There is also a case for developing a dedicated public programme focused on influencing attitudes to entrepreneurship among the populations from which high-value start-ups and scale-ups are most likely to come in advanced agriculture and biotechnology and food-for-the-future in Chiang Mai and Chiang Rai. In particular, this includes researchers and graduates in relevant university departments and managers of existing SMEs in the sectors. As well as awareness-raising on entrepreneurship opportunities and issues, policy needs to provide people from these populations with finance, help and incentives to change the mind-set of potential entrepreneurs to become aspirational and 'smart'. In particular, universities can play key roles in improving entrepreneurial culture, both by embedding high-quality teaching of entrepreneurship throughout the curriculum and through working on innovation and business development with local start-ups and scale-ups.

One of the key existing initiatives to promote an entrepreneurial culture is the Startup Thailand initiative, launched by the National Innovation Agency (NIA) in 2016[5]. It involves eight start-up ecosystem development programmes designed to build up awareness, increase ease of doing business, strengthen the ecosystem, and provide incentives and support. These programmes help start-ups to utilise local resources for their product and service development and help support entrepreneurship in potential driving sectors of Thailand's future growth ("locomotive" industries).[6] Programme 4 is entitled 'Startup regionalism'. This national initiative needs to be better exploited in the Northern region in order to develop grassroots communities, as has been the case with a the Startup Canada initiative (Box 2.3).

Box 2.3. Startup Canada

Description of the approach

Launched in 2012, Startup Canada is a national, entrepreneur-led, volunteer-run, not-for profit network organisation. It works to enhance the nation's competitiveness and prosperity by promoting a vibrant entrepreneurial culture and developing local entrepreneurial ecosystems. It has built a national network of hyper-connected startup communities, facilitated access for entrepreneurs to local sources of support and advice, and initiated high-impact national campaigns to fuel a culture of entrepreneurship across the country. It represents more than 200 000 entrepreneurs in 38 grassroots communities throughout Canada. It helps them to start, manage and scale up. Its main activities include digital programmes and flagship events, and through the Startup Canada Task Force, it influences national entrepreneurship policy. It also provides mentorship services to entrepreneurs, which have been identified as a major need.

Startup Canada Communities (SCC) is its flagship programme. It supports the connectivity, promotion and maturation of bottom-up entrepreneur-led communities across Canada. It started in 2013 with a pilot of 15 SCCs selected for their diversity of community size, demographics and industry sectors. This has now been extended to 38 SCCs. The SCCs provide a focus for the provision of frameworks; technology; branding; impact measurement and reporting tools; national working group sessions; access to leading advisors; national promotions; and connections with financiers and policy makers. Objectives include developing the regional infrastructure to strengthen Canada's entrepreneurial ecosystem and culture.

SCCs, led by local entrepreneurs in each community, are open to entrepreneurs of all types and at all stages of growth. At the local level, each member community acts as a point-of-entry for entrepreneurs in their local ecosystem, providing a connection to other start-up founders, and brokering access to mentors, space, funding opportunities, and support to start and grow their businesses. Communities do this through online resources as well as grassroots events that welcome, engage, and encourage all entrepreneurs. Each community's leaders also engage with local stakeholders in government and industry, as well as with investors, to form a partnership with a common goal of supporting the creation and growth of new companies locally. Because it is community-led, lack of trust is not an issue.

Entrepreneur leaders in each community secure a lead institutional partner with whom to co-chair regular Community Enterprise Partnership (CEP) meetings. CEPs are made up of local enterprise support stakeholders in each community – investor groups, incubators, accelerators, co-working spaces, support organisations, chambers, colleges, universities, associations, etc. Events like Startup Weekend, Startup Drinks and Demo Camp; and campaigns such as Global Entrepreneurship Week are typical events. SCCs provide regular opportunities for entrepreneurs to connect, learn-by-doing, and promote their ventures to the wider community. Local community leaders tap into the national network of communities across Canada and receive support and exposure through Startup Canada, for example through monthly online meet ups, websites, branding, guidelines, case studies and measurement tools.

The individual SCCs have begun to measure their impact and give feedback. Criteria for the assessment are: (1) accelerating the access of entrepreneurs to the support that they need; (2) starting and growing more successful start-up communities in terms of their infrastructure and level of activity; and (3) ecosystem maturation over time.

The 38 start-up communities are not equally active and many specialise. For example, Fredericton, New Brunswick, has specialised in fashion and lifestyle; Lloydminster, Alberta, primarily works to support entrepreneurs by offering business coaching, networking opportunities and professional learning events; and Moncton, New Brunswick, works closely with industry associations.

The Startup Canada Task Force is a platform to advance entrepreneurship policy in Canada. It aims to increase lack of national co-ordination and knowledge-sharing on entrepreneurship support. It brings together Canada's leading independent organisations representing venture capitalists, angel investors, business incubators, start-up accelerators and university research parks. The Task Force convenes entrepreneurs and cross-sector experts, liaises with government, and undertakes policy activities. It identifies priorities on a bi-annual basis.

The first annual **Startup Canada on the Hill** was held during Global Entrepreneurship Week in November 2013. It involved a large contingent of Canadian entrepreneurs going to Parliament Hill to for a national celebration of entrepreneurship together with the nation's elected representatives. This demonstrated the momentum, impact, and scale of the grassroots start-up movement in Canada engaged government in a discussion of its role in maximising entrepreneurial success.

The Startup Canada Women Entrepreneurs Program supports women entrepreneurs, particularly those from marginalised backgrounds, to start and scale thriving businesses. In 2020 Startup Canada in partnership with the Coca-Cola Foundation, supported 10 000 women entrepreneurs to start and scale thriving businesses through education, training, mentorship, support and resources.

The 2020 Social Impact Program, in partnership with the government's Investment Readiness Program (run by Economic and Social Development Canada), supports social entrepreneurs with access to training, mentorship, funding and resources to scale-up social and environmental impact. According to the 2020 Startup Canada Census, more than 40% of entrepreneurs are impact-driven and are interested in advancing the UN's Sustainable Development Goals. Every entrepreneur can sign up for the 2020 Social Impact Program for free to gain access to inspiration, recognition, support, training, funding and insights.

2020 Canadian Export Challenge. In 2020 Startup Canada, in collaboration with UPS and Export Development Canada, has invited entrepreneurs to join the challenge to become export-ready, connect with the trade and global growth system, and gain global exposure through a series of one-day accelerator events, digital programmes, pitch competitions, and an online community. It engages Canada's export and global growth ecosystem actors to support the 2020 Global Entrepreneurs Cohort of 15 000 entrepreneurs in global activities.

The Canie Awards recognise excellence in Canadian innovation and entrepreneurship in current and aspiring entrepreneurs, and promote social impact among start-ups and SMEs.

Relevance for Chiang Mai and Chiang Rai regions

Startup Canada offers three main lessons for advanced agriculture and biotechnology and food-for-the-future in the Chiang Mai and Chiang Rai regions:

First is the importance of the ambition and organisation of the trusted, nationally-linked, and locally-led Start-up Canada Communities (SCCs). They facilitate information flows and broker links between entrepreneurs and governmental and other opportunities. By having a broad base of members, they can provide mentoring and networking skills that are cross-cutting, developing an inclusive ecosystem. A startup community in advanced agriculture and biotechnology and food-for-the-future in Chiang Mai and Chiang Rai would help mobilise entrepreneurs and develop initiatives tailored to local industrial opportunities.

Second is the importance of the advocacy and feedback roles played by the Startup Canada Task Force. This feeds directly into national policy-making. This type of network would support the OSMEP in obtaining information on the needs, views and opportunities of ambitious entrepreneurs in Chiang Mai and Chiang Rai.

Third, the SCCs are inclusive and support women entrepreneurs for example. This type of network would help expand the talent base brought to bear for the development of advanced agriculture and biotechnology and food-for-the-future in Chiang Mai and Chiang Rai.

The Startup Canada approach is different to the existing Startup Thailand programme because it is locally rather than nationally-led so the lines of communication are upwards. As Startup Thailand recognises, 'the country needs to implement an area-based innovation economy'.

Sources of further information: https://www.startupcan.ca/about; https://www.startupcan.ca/ourwork/startup-canada-task-force ; http://startupfredericton.ca; https://www.startuplloyd.com/about.

A further option to support entrepreneurship in Chiang Mai and Chiang Rai is to harness the talents of the many highly-skilled and often entrepreneurial return migrants coming back from Bangkok and abroad for entrepreneurship. The OSMEP could introduce a programme providing some resources in order to organise and lubricate the processes of integrating those who are interested in entrepreneurship into the entrepreneurial ecosystem by funding awareness-raising, mentoring and networking activities. As has been found in the Czech Republic (Bernard et al., 2013), returnees have often acquired highly valuable knowledge and know-how as well as personal contacts for entrepreneurship projects. Their participation in social networks focused on entrepreneurship and involvement in entrepreneurship support initiatives is therefore desirable. They may wish to start businesses themselves, or they may be able to advise local entrepreneurs about opportunities using their networks and knowledge. Universities could facilitate this by leading in creating and maintaining networks of entrepreneurs and asking return migrants to speak to potential entrepreneurs, complementing the Entrepreneurial University programme introduced by ONES.

Networks

Networks are important for start-ups and scale-ups by giving access to knowledge about technologies, markets, suppliers, and other opportunities. They are also important to co-ordinating actors in developing and implementing a regional entrepreneurial ecosystem strategy.

There is an increasing number of networks and networking events in Chiang Mai and Chiang Rai, such as in tea and coffee, which support entrepreneurs and serve to raise the profile of the cluster nationally and internationally. However, there are also weaknesses in the networks related to:

- lack of involvement of larger companies and 'smart firms' in local networking activities;
- lack of engagement of universities in local networking activities, other than those set up by the universities or the NSP themselves;
- lack of trust between firms; and
- an absence of coordination of and between networks.

Thus a local policy intervention is needed to identify how the network provision can be strengthened, including how to incentivise relevant academics (and students) to play a full part in networks and how to support larger SMEs and entrepreneurs with links to university-based knowledge. A lead on co-ordination is also required.

Three types of networks operate in Chiang Mai and Chiang Rai that are relevant to advanced agriculture and biotechnology and food-for-the-future:

1. Networks of generic SME representative bodies and their regional sub-bodies – Chambers of Commerce and Federation of Thai Industries (FTI);
2. Sector-specific cross-boundary initiatives – Thailand Food Valley North; and
3. The national TCELS network and national networking bodies.

These are discussed below.

Chambers of Commerce and the Federation of Thai Industries

The Chambers of Commerce and the Federation of Thai Industries are important membership and networking organisations active in the Northern Region that also provide support for industry development. The Chamber of Commerce in Chiang Mai has 700-800 members in a range of sectors, with a weighting towards medium-sized firms. One of its main roles is export promotion for SMEs in conjunction with the OSMEP. The Federation of Thai Industries (FTI) is a non-profit organisation with government and private sector support. Its activities include a programme for the development of the agro-food industry start-ups, including financial support to acquire machinery and channels for on-line marketing. The FTI Biotech Industry Group in Chiang Mai has some 30 member companies, including about 20 companies which are relatively advanced. More than 100 are showing an interest in joining. However, in spite of FTI efforts to encourage larger healthcare companies to join the club, they have not yet joined.

There is an opportunity to make greater use of these networks to channel university research to start-ups and scale-ups in the advanced agriculture and biotechnology and food-for-the-future sectors. An example of good practice is the Innovation Longan project.[7] This is led by the FTI Chiang Mai Chapter with partnership from the Research and Development Innovation Service, NIA, and NSTDA Northern Network. Longan is one of the prize fruits grown in northern Thailand, especially in Lamphun province in Chiang Mai. The Innovation Longan project helps local SMEs to differentiate their products and access new markets exploiting active ingredients of longan – anti-oxidant and anti-carcinogenic nutrients suitable for medicine and supplementary foods – by introducing new product and process innovations researched by Chiang Mai, Maejo, Kasetsart and other universities. The initiative steers university research towards areas with business development feasibility and market potential and promotes market-oriented innovations to SMEs and investors. More projects of this kind could be developed.

Thailand Food Valley North

Thailand Food Valley is a cluster initiative with 300-400 member firms spanning small, micro and large companies. It includes a geographical focus in the north in the form of Thailand Food Valley North, which includes 'Command Centres' in Chiang Mai and Chiang Rai. The initiative includes networking among the members, as well as services for SMEs such as training in innovation, help to develop prototypes and product packaging through Chiang Mai University and government funding support for marketing, including sending entrepreneurs on study visits aboard, especially to the Netherlands. The project has an inclusive board representing key stakeholders in the food industry as well as provincial government authorities. It receives NIA funding and a grant from the JICA association. The Chiang Mai Command Centre is in the local office of the FTI, and has two full-time employees and many advisers.

The Food Valley initiative is not yet fully mature. The member firms work together but most of the companies are low tech, many of the entrepreneurs are in the early stages of development of their projects, the entrepreneurs are still not keen to work with universities and the public sector, a culture of collaboration among the firms is missing and there is no innovative 'anchor firm' for the network. The only major firm, Sunsweet (700 employees) was listed on the stock market in 2018. It undertakes contract farming and collaborates with other companies and has only recently begun to be more advanced in biotech, including starting an R&D department. In this context, more investment and budget is needed to support Food Valley to develop clear consistent plans, strong co-ordination, a professional management system, and co-investments and joint activities. Sunsweet has connections in 40 to 50 countries and could act as a potential anchor for the development of the whole cluster. Government funding will be needed as members are not yet at the stage of being able to finance the activities solely through paying membership fees.

The Thai Biotechnology Industry Association

The Thai Biotechnology Industry Association (ThaiBio) is a Bangkok-based national organisation that supports the country's biotechnology businesses to grow sustainably and achieve international competitiveness (http://www.thaibio.or.th). A regional branch covering Chiang Mai and Chiang Rai is needed. An international inspiring practice example is provided by One Nucleus, a local specialist network that was originally funded by a regional development agency in the east of England, United Kingdom (see Box 2.4).

Box 2.4. One Nucleus: A regional biotech and life science networking organisation, United Kingdom

Description of the approach

One Nucleus is a regional not-for-profit membership organisation specialising in Life Science, Healthcare, Biotechnology, and Medical Devices, operating on a fee-paying basis. While it was originally focused on the East of England and based in Cambridge, members of One Nucleus are drawn from the Greater London-Cambridge-East of England corridor, Europe's largest life sciences and healthcare cluster. It supports those institutions, companies and individuals undertaking activity in or with the region as a whole. It provides local, UK-wide and international connectivity helping its members to maximise their performance.

The network needed public funding in order to get established. It was originally set up in 1997 as the Eastern Region Biotechnology Initiative (ERBI), 50% funded by the national Government's Department of Trade and Industry. The rest of its funding came from membership subscriptions. Subsequently ERBI was part-funded by the Eastern Region Development Agency (EEDA) established in 1999, its first contribution to the Cambridge biotech cluster.

One of its activities involves face-to-face training programmes, including offering technical courses, for example in biosafety, laboratory health and safety, and introductory courses including introduction to contracts, drug development and on-line courses such as managing life science projects. Soft skill providers include specialist firms and the Welcome Sanger Institute (a research institute).

Networking is a key element in the activities of One Nucleus. Conferences and events provide a platform for business-to-business interactions. The event portfolio includes monthly networking opportunities at BioWednesdays in London and Cambridge, the Life Science Leadership Series, the annual Cambridge flagship event ON Helix and the flagship event Genesis in London.

Factors for success

Early outcomes of the network's activities included the development of a common pool of expertise, skilled labour, training services, laboratory space and marketing activities. However, collaboration for drug development was less common amongst the region's firms. As the bioscience sector grew, so did the demand for networking and business support activities. By the mid-2000s, ERBI (2006) identified that there were some 200 biotech companies and 350 biotech expertise service providers, plus research institutes and universities and 20 multinationals in pharmaceuticals, agri-bio and food as well as 4 hospitals involved in biotech research.

The key factor for success of the network was the initial funding provided by the UK government and subsequent funding at the regional level. Early national and then regional funding enabled the formation of networks and formal links between the wide range of member organisations. Without public funding there would have been little capacity to broker such interactions, for a networking culture to develop and for the international promotion of the cluster.

Public sector intervention also broadened the scope of ERBI's operations and its role as a central actor in the cluster. For example, Medilink East, supported by EEDA, has been providing a range of services and support to companies in the medical technology sector since 1998. With further support from EEDA, the service was taken over by ERBI with the intention of improving and expanding the services offered. With public support, ERBI was able to extend its operations internationally as well as nationally. In 2009, ERBI made an agreement with the Massachusetts Biotech Council (MassBio) to encourage and promote the biotechnology industry in both regions – Massachusetts USA and Oxford, London and Cambridge, UK. In April 2010, ERBI merged with the London Bioscience Network (LBN). It was renamed One Nucleus in June 2010.

Obstacles encountered and responses

Obstacles faced by the network were caused by changes in the political system. In 2010 it was announced that the English regional development agencies (RDAs), including EEDA the sponsor of the network, were to be abolished. They were closed in 2012. The principal duty on RDAs was to draw up and keep under constant review a 5 to 10-year Regional Economic Strategy. Without this regional strategy, ERBI/One Nucleus lost funding and regional support. Its response was to expand its membership base and increase the range of its paying services. Merging with LBN also gave it a much stronger base from which to work. This included incorporating a very strong bioscience cluster and one which included headquarters of United Kingdom and international pharmaceutical companies. It also meant that it had better access to finance providers based in London that could be linked with members. Hence it operates a dual strategy of London as well as Cambridge activities. The merger also enabled the Cambridge operation to overcome a problem of being seen to be parochial and isolated.

Relevance for Chiang Mai and Chiang Rai regions

This case demonstrates how public funding established and supported the early and later growth stages of a biotechnology members' network that became very important to fostering collaboration, strategy development, training and research services and building the international profile of a region in biotechnology. It was national funding that got the network started and regional funding that enabled a regional response to the needs of a rapidly growing sector. The national and regional funding enabled the network to become established as the central and most important actor in the cluster.

A similar networking initiative could be built in Chiang Mai and Chiang Rai. It could include services for start-ups and scale-ups in biotech that actively develop the supply chain and open up export markets. A network of this kind could also play a critical role in linking its members to national centres of finance in Bangkok, and in building the international profile of advanced agriculture and biotechnology and food-for-the-future in the North of Thailand. This regional network would build a stronger basis for international sales, research collaborations, inward FDI and so on. The long time period that it takes for a network of this kind to reach maturity should be noted, together with the importance of making a start even from modest beginnings.

Sources of further information: https://www.theengineer.co.uk/boost-for-easts-medtech-firms; https://sciencebusiness.net/news/68785/UK-biotech-bodies-to-collaborate-with-MassBio.

Thailand Centre of Excellence for Life Sciences

The Thailand Centre of Excellence for Life Sciences (TCELS) is a national initiative based in Bangkok, which includes networking for life sciences firms, together with mentoring and consultancy for SMEs, training for entrepreneurs in areas such as IP protection, and support in connecting firms to organisations that can help with access to finance. It also funds university research to develop technology to strengthen the life science ecosystem, including research with potential for start-ups and licensing, and uses a database for matching businesses to university research opportunities. It also approaches university lecturers in relevant subjects to be unpaid mentors, and has identified mentors in Chiang Mai and Chiang Rai universities. In one of its projects, TCELS works with NSP on a digital health cluster with funding from the OSMEP.

To build its network, TCELS is attempting to find an organisation in each region to act as a focal point and to recruit members. In 2019, it had no member companies in Chiang Mai or Chiang Rai. An option for building networking for advanced agriculture and life sciences firms in Chiang Mai and Chiang Rai is therefore to support the development of a stronger regional branch of TCELS.

Overall, establishing global, regional and local collaborative networks is a key goal of the Thailand 4.0 Strategy (Maesincee, 2018). The various programmes discussed here are designed to build networks of entrepreneurs and SMEs that can share infrastructure and technology and have access to R&D and consulting services. However, there are too many government organisations with the same or similar goals working independently with little collaboration. An overall lead network would help bring together the key members and services.

Conclusions and policy recommendations

There is strong potential for the development of the advanced agriculture and biotechnology and food-for-the-future sectors in the Chiang Mai and Chiang Rai regions, which will support the development of key strategic industries for the Thai economy as a whole. However, future development of the sectors in these regions requires more start-ups and especially scale-ups. There are both strengths and weaknesses in the regional entrepreneurial ecosystem in this respect. The priority areas to address in terms of overcoming bottlenecks and releasing more innovative entrepreneurship are the pillars of the regional entrepreneurial ecosystem concerned with access to finance, regional entrepreneurial talent and skills, entrepreneurial culture, and networks. In addition, specific measures can be promoted in other areas. The key policy recommendations in line with this agenda are set out below. The OSMEP is ideally suited to lead by providing plans, quality control, incentivising people and organisations to take part and targeting public financial support to give maximal leverage.

Box 2.5. Recommendations on the regional entrepreneurial ecosystem

1. Actions in key priority pillars of the regional entrepreneurial ecosystem:

Finance

- Increase targeting of public SME finance support programmes to start-ups and scale-ups with clearly identified and articulated growth potential in strategic sectors for Thai economic growth.
- Combine the offer of finance with advice and mentoring support to start-ups and scale-ups.
- Promote a crowdfunding initiative for start-ups and scale-ups in the Northern region.
- Develop an angel network for the Northern region.

Talent and skills

- Involve the regional universities, especially their business schools, in identifying technical, business, managerial and other skills needed in start-ups and scale-ups in advanced agriculture and biotechnology and food-for-the-future in Chiang Mai and Chiang Rai.
- Improve university teaching of these skills through upskilling staff, updating curricula, and involving practitioners in the teaching, especially those with wide or international experience.
- Promote new models of teaching and new teaching targets at university level to address start-up and scale-up needs, e.g. through advanced apprenticeship programmes, internships, Masters dissertations on industry relevant problems, technology-supported classrooms onsite at a scale up or "Faculty on the Shop Floor" programmes.
- Expand initiatives to create and support serial entrepreneurs; involve them in supporting further entrepreneurship in regions; and publicise them as role models for entrepreneurs through support centres and web presences.

Entrepreneurial culture

- Instigate a programme for raising awareness of entrepreneurship and supporting entrepreneurial culture changing activities. It should include:
  - Involving successful entrepreneurial return migrants and alumni in university entrepreneurship support programmes so that the relevant knowledge is disseminated.
  - Promoting internships in existing SMEs by university students with an ambition to innovate and take the SME forward.
  - Sensitivity to gender differences so that especially females have support tailored to their needs.

Networks

- Allocate sustained, predictable funding for the establishment and operation of an overarching advanced agriculture and biotechnology and food-for-the-future networking organisation in Chiang Mai and Chiang Rai, potentially building on one of the existing networks.
- The networking organisation should include private sector and university members, and offer a range of services as well as networking events, such as consultancy, training, research and connections to financing opportunities. It should also raise the national and international visibility of the region's activities, and can be connected to a wider national network.

2. Actions in other areas of the entrepreneurial ecosystem

Connectivity infrastructure

- Improve ICT bandwidth outside the main cities so that SMEs can use higher speeds.
- Provide digital training and support for new SME digital users.

Demand for relevant products

- Offer start-ups and scale-ups competitive grants and an advice service delivered through third parties in activities which improve product quality, direct exporting and participation in global value chains.
- Develop and institute a national product quality trade mark to be awarded to start-ups and scale-ups with safe products to support their branding of quality.
- Create a healthcare innovation procurement initiative involving a range of government ministries, agencies and healthcare providers in Chiang Mai and Chiang Rai. Agencies could give a minimum share (say 10%) of their public procurement projects related to advanced agriculture and biotechnology and food-for-the-future to new firms, so that these start-ups can create profiles for later bidding in future government projects. Subsequent project funding could then focus on scaling up activities.

Business services

- Strengthen the OSMEP One Stop Shops by supporting staff training and increasing their funding so that they can act as key hubs with a coordinating role bringing start-ups and scale-ups with common problems together to develop shared or joint solutions.
- Select start-ups and potential scale-up SMEs for business advice support according to their absorptive capacity.

Access to knowledge

- Organise links between universities for shared research commercialisation infrastructure, for example by providing some network funding for training and support to start-ups and scale-ups in establishing and protecting IP.
- Expand funding and provide long-term budgets to universities in Chiang Mai and Chiang Rai for applied research projects relevant to the needs of start-ups and scale-ups in advanced agriculture and biotechnology and food-for-the-future.
- Build R&D absorption capacity in SMEs by providing innovation grants and loans.
- Involve retired entrepreneurs as mentors for ambitious start-ups and scale-ups, rewarding the entrepreneurs by prestige and/or finance.

Ecosystem leadership

- Produce and implement regional entrepreneurial ecosystem development strategy document for the development of advanced agriculture and biotechnology and food-for-the-future in Chiang Mai and Chiang Rai. This should include collaboration among national and provincial government agencies, universities, science parks, research laboratories, and businesses.

Regulations

- Support SMEs going through FDA approval in Thailand through a properly staffed designated lead organisation, such as the Federation of Thai Industries. This support needs to be knowledgeable, timely, and address the common issues that currently cause delays and failures.

References

Arunmas, P. (2019), "Cutting through the gloom in export prospects," 1 July, Bangkok Post, Bangkok, Thailand, https://www.bangkokpost.com/business/1704820/cutting-through-the-gloom-in-export-prospects/

Bernard, J., V. Patockova and T. Kostelecky (2013), "Islands of Innovation in the Czech Republic: the international labour markets of highly skilled workers and brain gain policies", in U. Hilpert and H. Lawton Smith (eds) *Networking Regionalised Innovative Labour Markets*, Routledge, London.

Beveridge, L. (2001), *Cambridge Entrepreneurs: In the business of technology*, Granta Editions, Cambridge, UK.

Chong, C. (2019), "Keep calm and carrot on: how agritech could transform farming in Singapore." 19 January, *sgsme.sg*, Singapore Press Holdings Ltd., Singapore

Cohen, W. M. and D. A. Levinthal (1990), "Absorptive capacity: A new perspective on learning and innovation", *Administrative Science Quarterly*, 35(1), 128-152.

Guelich, U. (2018), Global Entrepreneurship Monitor (GEM), *Thailand Report, 2017/2018*, Bangkok University, Bangkok, Thailand.

Hoogenberg, D. (2020), "How biotech scale ups can contribute to the health industry transformation", EY Netherlands, Rotterdam, https://www.ey.com/en_nl/health/how-biotech-scale-ups-can-contribute-to-the-health-industry-transformation/

Maesincee, S. (2018), "Thailand's Transformation through Science Technology Innovation," 19 March, presentation by H.E. Dr Suvit Maesincee, Minister of Science and Technology, Thailand.

Magnin, C. (2016), *How big data will revolutionize the global food chain*, McKinsey & Company, New York City, USA

OECD (2019), Local Entrepreneurship Ecosystems and Emerging Industries: Case Study of Coventry and Warwickshire, United Kingdom, OECD Local Economic and Employment Development Working Paper, OECD Publishing, Paris.

Politis, D. (2008), "Business Angels and value added: what do we know and where do we go?", *Venture Capital: International Journal of Entrepreneurial Finance*, 10(2), 127-147 https://www.researchgate.net/publication/247518655_Business_Angels_and_Value_Added_What_Do_We_Know_and_Where_Do_We_Go/.

World Bank (2018), *International LPI: Global Rankings 2018*, World Bank, Washington DC, USA.

Notes

[1] A scale-up company is defined by the OECD as one that has average annualised growth of at least 10% in turnover or employment in the previous 3 years, starting with at least 10 employees at the beginning of the period.

[2] Data are not directly comparable with other countries, but in OECD countries the share of firms with 50-249 employees averages 1.7% of the firm population.

[3] http://web.nso.go.th/en/survey/bts/datafiles/2014_n_bts_Executive%20Summary.pdf

[4] https://www.todayonline.com/world/thailand-plans-trans-asean-bullet-train-linking-china-laos-and-even-singapore

[5] See https://uuku.fi/insights/thailands-leap-towards-a-digital-economy/.

[6] https://www.managementcentre.co.uk/developing-business-model-canvas/

[7] https://cpduk.co.uk/news-articles/view/continuing-professional-development-for-universities

[8] http://www.bbk.ac.uk/study/2019/postgraduate/programmes/TMSBIOBS_C/

[9] http://www.biotec.or.th/en/images/document/1.pdf

[1] https://www.nstda.or.th/thailandtechshow/2019/

[2] http://cor.europa.eu/en/documentation/studies/Documents/Forstering_innovation_EER.pdf (accessed January 12 2017

[3] https://angel.co/thailand/investors.

[4] See https://www.facebook.com/pg/ChiangMaiEntrepreneurs/about/?ref=page_internal.

[5] https://startupthailand.org/st2019/

[6] https://www.startupthailand.org/wp-content/uploads/2018/11/white-paper.pdf

[7] http://www.value-chains.org/dyn/bds/docs/497/Vichien_ChiangMaiInnovation.pdf

Annex 2.A. SWOT analysis

Annex Table 2.A.1. Pillars of the Chiang Mai and Chiang Rai regional entrepreneurial ecosystem for advanced agriculture and biotechnology and food-for-the-future

Connectivity infrastructure	
Strengths	*Weaknesses*
Location for cross-border trade	Technology infrastructure
	High logistics costs
	Inefficient supply chains
Opportunities	*Threats*
Government spending on infrastructure	
Digital Thailand initiative	
Smart City in Chiang Mai	
Demand for products	
Strengths	*Weaknesses*
Agri-tech and biotech still in very early stages of growth	Products easy to replicate / copy
Demand from China	
Good raw materials for advanced agriculture and biotechnology and food-for-the-future	
Opportunities	*Threats*
Large market opportunity domestic and international	Limited anti-monopoly regulations make it hard to compete with larger Thai conglomerates with distribution
Trends towards healthier and medicinal foods	
Development of higher value products	
Branding the Chiang Mai/Chiang Rai cluster	
Innovative public procurement to stimulate healthy foods	
Business services	
Strengths	*Weaknesses*
Serviced-minded culture	Most suppliers very centralised in Bangkok or other big cities
Multiple sources of public business services support	Poor quality and consistency in public business development services
Availability of private sector business advice	Limited emphasis of public business advice on growth SMEs
	Lack of targeted and intense support for innovative scale ups
Opportunities	*Threats*
Increase quality and professionalisation in government business services	
Increase use of vouchers for innovation consultancy	
Collective action for business services	
Talent and skills	
Strengths	*Weaknesses*
Creative, self-reliant	Outdated university training programmes
Networking skills, social media skills	Family business mind-set - weak on branding and export
STEM graduates from regional universities	Worker skill shortages
	Culture of not wanting to be first
	Fear of failure highest in ASEAN
	Brain drain
	Lack of serial entrepreneurs
Opportunities	*Threats*
University business school support for SME management development	Entrepreneurial culture of copying what is successful rather than innovating
Getting more technical experts in various fields	

Better quality of life in Chiang Mai, Chiang Rai	
University-industry mobility schemes	
Access to knowledge	
Strengths	*Weaknesses*
Access to R&D and IP	Low absorptive capacity of SMEs
Collaboration with universities reducing development costs	Lack of FDI and large firm anchors for knowledge exchange
NSP translating knowledge to industry	
Opportunities	*Threats*
Track and measure progress from all incubation activities with SMEs	
Maintain active databases on knowledge and allow SME users to access	
Ecosystem leadership	
Strengths	*Weaknesses*
Government S-curve strategy	Lack of regional tailoring of policies
Multiple government agencies supporting ecosystem	Tick box mentality of programme managers
Strong anchor organisations in universities and science park	Government KPIs not focused on entrepreneurship and SME success
	Lack of large firm leaders
Opportunities	*Threats*
Creation of a cluster management organisation	
Finance	
Strengths	*Weaknesses*
Breadth and number of public programmes for SMEs	Difficult and costly to access bank loans without collateral
Foreign and domestic venture capital is available	Most government schemes are 'first come-first served'
	Small range of financial instruments
	Little targeting of government programmes to innovative start-ups
	Not enough complementary advice
	Limited business angel funding
Opportunities	*Threats*
Build credit ratings of individuals and SMEs	Technology bringing more efficient and cheaper ways to access funds
Share and repeat success stories	
Make SMEs more aware of existing programmes	
Favourable context of new crowdfunding regulations	
Regulations	
Strengths	*Weaknesses*
SEZ Food Innopolis on NSP facilitating R&D intensive investments	Slow and uncertain FDA regulatory approval process
	Weak IP protection and legal framework
Opportunities	*Threats*
Government aims to make the overall system more transparent	Lack of continuity between government administrations. Programmes lose funding after 4-5 years
	Most SMEs cannot survive a legal challenge
	Too many government agencies with overlapping goals
	Lack of co-ordination between government agencies

Entrepreneurial culture	
Strengths	*Weaknesses*
Positive attitudes to entrepreneurship in the population	Copy other successful business models rather than innovate
Opportunity perception is high	Afraid to fail
	Low share of women entrepreneurs
Opportunities	*Threats*
Training to reduce fear of failure	More tech-savvy countries like Malaysia, Singapore, and India competing in the biotechnology and agri-tech sectors
Potential for more growth entrepreneurship among women	
Highly-skilled and entrepreneurial returning migrants	

Stimulation of more entrepreneurs from university students	
Networks	
Strengths	*Weaknesses*
Multiple existing cluster initiatives	Fragmented networks
BOI incentives for clusters and SEZ	Lack of sustainable finance for networks
	Limited critical mass of biotech scale ups
Opportunities	*Threats*
Create an overarching cluster network	

Source: Authors

3 Business development services

This chapter examines how to strengthen business development services for start-ups and scale-ups in the Chiang Mai and Chiang Rai advanced agriculture and biotechnology and food-for-the-future cluster. It covers advice, consultancy, mentoring and management training. It starts by proposing avenues for improving business development services in Thailand, including by creating a more integrated business development services system, developing more online support, introducing a voucher system and expanding mentoring. It then focuses on creating a new "fast-track" strand of support for start-ups and scale-ups with innovation and exporting potential. Features include connections with private suppliers, a client-centred approach, and a structure to co-ordinate business development services suppliers in the cluster. The role of business incubators in business advice is also briefly discussed. The chapter ends with conclusions and recommendations.

Introduction

Business development services (BDS) can be broadly defined as services that aim to improve the performance of user enterprise, for example its access to markets and its ability to compete. They may refer to information, training, consultancy and advisory services, marketing assistance, technology development and transfer, and business linkages promotion (Committee of Donor Agencies for Small Enterprise Development, 2001).

Governments take different approaches to meeting the BDS needs of start-ups and scale-ups (OECD, 2020). Providing a full range of services through a network of public institutions is a valid option in certain conditions. This is most relevant when private sector consultancy services in the country are underdeveloped, when there is lack of availability or access for start-ups and scale-ups to these private services, or when the nature of the services is not fully sensitive to the needs of start-ups and scale-ups. However, if the market of external consultants is relatively well-developed, public services may crowd-out the private sector, which should be avoided (OECD, 2017).

Government policies can add value to existing BDS offers in various ways, in particular by providing financial support to start-ups and scale-ups to encourage their use of the services, helping firms to understand their business needs through an initial company diagnostic, and referring firms to service providers of proven quality relevant to the type of services needed (OECD, 2017, 2018a).

The role of an SME agency in the provision of BDS will differ depending on the market conditions affecting the access of SMEs to private sector services. Most commonly, governments adopt a mixed approach whereby the government delivers some of the services, usually basic information and advisory services, and draws on private sector expertise to provide more sophisticated technical advice and assistance. In the mixed approach, governments may partner with private and/or civil society organisations (e.g. universities, chambers of commerce) to extend the reach of BDS to SMEs in local communities or to special target groups. For example, the US Small Business Administration (SBA) has service level agreements with about 1 000 university-based Small Business Development Centres (SBDCs) to deliver BDS to entrepreneurs and SMEs in their geographic areas. It would be unusual for a government in any country to rely on the private BDS market as the sole source of advisory and consultancy services to SMEs, but the role of the private sector can grow as it is supported by the government, as has been the case in Indonesia for example (see Box 3.1).

Box 3.1. Recent evolution of business development services in Indonesia

The initial policy of the Indonesian government was to encourage a supply of private sector BDS providers by providing a small amount of initial operational capital to private sector consultants who would agree to provide various BDS services to SMEs. However, the quality of the consultants was uneven and often unpredictable, thus causing strong heterogeneity in the quality of services to SMEs across the country. Furthermore, most consultants were based in large urban areas, leaving SMEs in many parts of Indonesia underserved or unserved. Finally, in a system where only part of the services cost was covered by the government, most consultants preferred working with larger SMEs which could pay more, thus leaving smaller SMEs underserved.

In 2013, the Ministry of Cooperatives and SMEs sought to improve co-ordination and standardisation of BDS across Indonesia by launching the "Integrated Business Services Centres" (PLUT-KUMKM). The main objective was to make comprehensive, integrated and affordable (free) BDS available to SMEs through a network of local one-stop shops. These one-stop shops developed relationships with private-sector organisations and qualified consultants/advisors with strong BDS expertise to deliver the services. This approach had the advantage of creating a local demand for BDS, leveraging existing private sector expertise, and minimising the negative effects from the possible crowding-out of the private sector consultancy industry

Source: OECD (2018b)

It is common for governments to make use of approved consultants and mentors as part of subsidised programmes to improve SMEs' access to private sector BDS. However, it is important that the intermediaries and external consultants are appropriately skilled, have incentives to supply high-quality services, and that their consultancy interventions are perceived by SMEs to be beneficial. At the same time, co-ordination and quality control can be very important considerations in the outsourcing of publicly-supported BDS services.

Business development services policy in Thailand needs to take a differentiated approach, which distinguishes between a track of generic and basic business development services support for all SMEs and a track of more intensive business development services combined with financial and innovation support for start-ups and scale-ups with innovation and exporting potential in driving sectors for the future development of the Thai economy, including advanced agriculture and biotechnology and food-for-the-future in Chiang Mai and Chiang Rai. The latter is likely to require a shift from a system dominated by direct public sector provision of BDS, to a public sector role that is more focused on stimulating SME demand for BDS by providing incentives such as vouchers, acting as a broker between supply and demand, and ensuring good performance of publicly-subsidised BDS supply, for example with performance management systems and support for capacity-building of consultants and BDS suppliers.

Strengthening business development services in Thailand

Increasing integration in the system for referring SMEs to BDS suppliers

Thailand has an extensive system of business support centres and mechanisms for providing policy support to SMEs. They include the OSMEP One-Stop Shops (OSSs), SME Support and Rescue Centres (SSRCs), Business Support Centres (BSCs), and branch offices of the SME Development Bank and the Industrial Estate Authority of Thailand. In 2017, this comprised a network of 248 locations nationwide (JICA/UNICO International Cooperation, 2018). However, more efforts are needed to refer SMEs to the right BDS supports in the network. A number of key tools can be used for this – the RISMEP referral system, the OSMEP one-stop shop centres, the OSMEP SME ONE web portal, and a potential new digital business diagnostic tool. It is important to maintain and strengthen the existing tools in these areas and fill the gaps in the system.

The RISMEP client referral system

The Regional Integrated SME Promotion (RISMEP) project was funded by the Japan International Cooperation Agency (JICA) from 2009 to 2018. As a result of the project, about a third of Thailand's provinces have developed an integrated and collaborative "referral" system for servicing the needs of SMEs (see Box 3.2). Based on this initial success, the Thai government allocated funding to expand the RISMEP mechanism to all provinces by 2023, increasing the number from 22 provinces in 2019 to 44 in 2021 and to the remainder over the following two years.[1] This roll out will be important in strengthening business development services across Thailand.

Box 3.2. Overview of the RISMEP project in Thailand

RISMEP was the outcome of an agreement between the Ministry of Industry and the Japan International Cooperation Agency (JICA), implemented by the Industrial Promotion Centres (IPCs) with technical assistance and funding from JICA between 2009 and 2018.

In provinces implementing the RISMEP mechanism, entrepreneurs and SMEs can approach any of the one-stop shop "consultation counters", have their questions answered, and be referred to the most appropriate partner organisation for follow-up BDS support based on a simple diagnostic.

A core feature of the mechanism is the formation of a business development service providers' network in each province. Network members include the one-stop shops (OSS), government offices, SME support organisations, independent consultants, financial institutions, chambers of commerce and industry, the Federation of Thai Industries (FTI), SME associations, and university lecturers. The creation of these networks produces a more horizontal, integrated approach to servicing the BDS needs of start-ups and SMEs. As a connecting point between the network of BDS-providing organisations and SMEs, the one-stop shops are able to facilitate efficient matching of suitable services to the needs of specific SMEs.

The matching process is facilitated by use of the Japanese-developed Shindan "awakening tool" promoted by the RISMEP approach for use by the OSS consultation service counters in performing a preliminary diagnosis of the business needs of the SME clients.

The matching process is further aided by an organised database system that contains information on the business development service providers and their services. This facilitates referrals to the appropriate support services, or combination thereof, based on the needs of SME clients first approaching the OSS Centres and the use of local service providers.

The business development services providers in the RISMEP networks have also expanded the availability of their services to SMEs by accepting online consultations and having websites, thus improving their overall BDS practices (becoming more demand-driven).

In the future roll-out of the RISMEP approach, additional efforts may be needed to overcome some of the remaining barriers to co-ordination of providers that had not yet been addressed at the closing of the JICA project in 2018, such as improvements to the service co-ordination skills of the one-stop consultation services centres and wider application of the know-how and tools of the RISMEP model (JICA/UNICO International Cooperation, 2018). More efforts are also required to promote the merits of joint collaboration among the agencies operating one-stop consultation centres in order to provide a more integrated approach to helping SMEs solve their business and technology development problems. Increasing this level of collaboration would enable the OSS services centres to more fully deploy comprehensive support functions.

Sustainability of the RISMEP mechanism will also require ongoing efforts to expand the number of business development services provider network members, particularly private sector consultants, provide training for new members in the approach, tools (e.g. use of the Shindan diagnostic tool) and counselling skills, and continue to strengthen the capacity of network members to deliver appropriate referral and the "team consulting" approach through information sharing.

OSMEP one-stop shops

The OSMEP one-stop shops and the Department of Industrial Promotion (DIP) Business Support Centres and SSRCs have a presence in all 77 provinces. They have a significant reach to SMEs, having provided 178 304 services to an estimated 63 604 SMEs in 2019.[2] They provide basic advice to local SMEs directly, and connect SMEs to the technology programmes of other ministries and agencies, regional science parks, university incubation centres, and networks of BDS-providing organisations and private sector consultants for technical assistance and more sophisticated BDS.

OSMEP SME One web portal

In 2018, the OSMEP launched the SME One web portal (www.smeone.info) as an all-in-one web-based information service about SME support agencies and programmes in Thailand. It involves a co-operative initiative between the OSMEP and the Export-Import Bank of Thailand, including Memorandums of Understanding (MOUs) with 69 state and private organisations and financial institutions. SME One aims to support SMEs with access to useful information for the development and expansion of their businesses by providing knowledge, "tips" for starting and growing a business, and linkages with a wide range of services, as well as being a window for SMEs to search and register for services and apply to participate in activities.

There is scope to strengthen the portal. Currently the portal allows users to search for SME service centres (e.g. incubators) that might be able to address their challenges or needs. However it falls short of providing links to information on key support programmes, such as programmes of the National Science and Technology Agency (NSTDA) or the National Innovation Agency (NIA). Further, the site is not directly linked to the OSMEP website (www.sme.go.th) nor does it integrate pertinent key OSMEP resources, such as the SME Knowledge Centre (www.smeknowledgecenter.com) and the new OSMEP SME Regular Level Promotion and Development Programme to support businesses in realising their potential and upgrading their business and product standards[3].

To be a comprehensive one-stop SME portal, SME One should have links to all relevant sources of information. Examples of well-developed SME portals from Israel and the United States are highlighted in Box 3.3.

Box 3.3. Comprehensive online SME information and resource portals: examples from Israel and the USA

Israel

In Israel, the Small and Medium Business Agency (SMBA) has established a One-Stop Shop SME Programme Information Portal (www.sba.org.il). The portal is an integrated, comprehensive "one-stop shop" that provides nascent and existing entrepreneurs with regular updates of government schemes, events and notices; guides relevant to legal issues (e.g. incorporation, partnerships, lease agreements), marketing and sales (e.g. marketing planning), accountancy issues (e.g. compliance issues with the government), etc.; and other practical tools, such as business plan calculators. It also provides a detailed and comprehensive search engine providing information on governmental and non-governmental finance and advice schemes, an online database of consultants (and forms to apply for highly-subsidised consultancy fees), online training courses (some free and others highly subsidised), and signposts/links to local SME support centres and other support providers (e.g. the Israeli Chamber of Commerce). Backed up by a mobile phone app, its own YouTube channel and a Facebook page, the portal makes access widely and conveniently available.

USA

The U.S. Small Business Administration (SBA) operates a well-organised online SME information resource (https://www.sba.gov/business-guide). The site provides guides and "how-to" instructions under four major headings reflecting the lifecycle stages of a business: Planning your business, Launching your business, Managing your business, and Growing your business. It also provides links to funding programmes and local assistance centres. In addition, it provides access to the SBA Learning Centre, an online training service that offers free online courses on a range of business topics related to the stages of business development (www.sba.gov/learning centre). Consisting of video tutorials, templates, and interactive assessments, these courses give entrepreneurs knowledge and tools to assist their business. It aims to support 300 000 clients in 2020 and 400 000 clients in 2021 (SBA, 2020). The SBA encourages its network of volunteer business mentors to also use these online learning course in their small business support efforts.

Sources:
Israel Small and Medium Business Agency (SMBA):https://www.sba.org.il/hb/Pages/default.aspx; US Small Business Administration (SBA): https://www.sba.gov/business-guide; www.sba.gov/learning-center; SBA (2020), "FY 2021 Congressional Justification and FY 2019 Annual Performance Report", U.S. Small Business Administration, Washington, DC, https://www.sba.gov/document/report--congressional-budget-justification-annual-performance-report

An online business diagnostic tool

A widely-used digital business diagnostic tool would be a further important part of an effective business development services system in Thailand. Such tools are important both in motivating the take up of business advice among SMEs and in steering SMEs towards the most appropriate sources of advice (OECD, 2018a). Digital diagnostic tools seek to give SME managers a framework to reflect upon different aspects of their company's performance and practices, such as their innovation strategy or human resources development, and signpost them to appropriate and tailored online or face-to-face advice.

A business diagnostic tool is included within the RISMEP project, based on the Shindan enterprise diagnosis method. This has been predominantly for face-to-face use, but is now also available to be used online by SMEs. The use of the tool is linked to the assignment of the appropriate business advisors and support by the OSMEP OSS consultation service. These advisors make use of the preliminary online diagnosis and/or of a more detailed face-to-face discussion with a OSS consultation service advisor.

With the planned roll-out of RISMEP to all Thai provinces, this online diagnostic tool can be a key part of the methodology for increasing the integration of the business development services system. However, some face-to-face interactions with an advisor may need to be retained to help the SME with interpreting the online results and considering next steps. The assessment results of a well-designed online diagnostic tool could provide linkages to training tools (such as the online SME Knowledge Centre) or SME support advice centres. In addition, an option could be made available to direct the SMEs to a private provider to discuss the self-assessment results.

In Vietnam, for example, the "business health check" diagnostic tool is a strong feature of the National SME Support Portal. SMEs can complete a self-assessment of their internal capabilities in 10 areas of their business (e.g. marketing, leadership, personnel, financial management, work productivity, etc.) and immediately receive a report indicating the areas of the business most in need of attention. The Vietnam Agency for Enterprise Development is addressing the issue of follow-up discussion of the results through a partnership with a private coaching firm whereby an SME manager completing the online assessment can request a free one-hour appointment with a "Business Coaching Expert" to discuss the results and receive advice and direction.

Expanding and strengthening the network of private consultants

As the BDS system becomes more mature in Thailand, it is appropriate to increase the share of publicly-subsidised services being delivered by private consultants as opposed to public employees. There are three main aspects to this – developing a database of private sector BDS suppliers that is unified across different government ministries and agencies, increasing quality control of third-party providers and developing a voucher system to enable users to spend credits with approved BDS providers.

Increasing the number of consultants in government BDS databases

A first standard step in the process of engaging private-sector suppliers for government-sponsored BDS internationally is putting out a call to private consultants or consultancy firms to express their interest in participating. They will need to complete an application form requesting detailed information on the consultant's expertise, areas of competency, and consultancy record. Consultants can then be selected and included in a database of approved suppliers to the publicly-supported programmes. Defining the selection criteria for inclusion in the database is important to this process, as quality is a key concern. A system for matching of SMEs to an appropriate consultant for the subsidised service must also be developed, as well as a process for approving subsidised assignments, and establishment of a quality control system for monitoring the delivery of the service and assessing the performance of the consultant in delivering the service to the SME client.

These processes have already been followed in Thailand for a number of programmes, but need to be developed more widely across programmes and agencies. In addition, there is scope to increase the sharing of information on private sector suppliers across programmes. For example, the OSMEP one-stop consultation counters have a database of private sector business advice suppliers in provinces covered by the RISMEP initiative. The NSTDA ITAP programme also has a network of over 1 500 professional technology experts[4] who can be called upon to assist innovative SMEs with their technology needs, and the NSTDA IDE4SME programme also makes use of external technology experts and mentors, drawn from a variety of local and overseas sources, to provide in-depth consultancy to innovation-driven SMEs.

A master database of the private BDS-providing organisations and consultants, organised by area of competence by province, should be constructed and made available to all consultation counters and network members. This will require maintaining an up-to-date mapping of the network of BDS-providing organisations and independent consultants in the region, according to their specialties and offerings, and mobilising the network to become familiar with the range and scope of each one's focus, capability and areas of competency.

Strengthening the quality of BDS consultants

Quality management is a key issue when expanding the network of private suppliers for publicly-subsidised BDS. One of the key issues is providing appropriate training for the consultants not just in the technical areas of the business, such as IT or marketing, but also in counselling and mentoring methods. Currently, private sector BDS consultants in Thailand often follow management consultancy training courses offered on a commercial basis by Thai universities, colleges and training institutions. However, these courses are not subject to the rigour, standardised curriculum, assessment, or governmental authorisation of the Japanese Shindan System introduced in Thailand in 1999[5] and tend to focus on individual areas of business (e.g. marketing, finance) and less on counselling intervention skills. Thus, they are not producing business consultants as experts with broad knowledge and diagnostic competencies.

Certification of business development consultants is another important element of the approach needed. The OSMEP could assume a leadership role in promoting the establishment of an organisation for certifying the qualifications of consultants offering BDS to SMEs as part of government-subsidised advice and counselling programmes.[6] This could possibly be developed in partnership with the Institute for SME Development (ISMED). The organisation could encompass development of standardised training programmes, supervision of training activities, and implementation of registration and certification schemes. Such a standards and certification approach is illustrated by the example from Poland (Box 3.4).

The RISMEP project also offers a model that can be used more widely in Thailand to strengthen the quality of BDS providers. It has provided guidance manuals on the delivery of consultation services[7], consulting service tools, and training to consultants in business counsellor techniques. It also includes a certification system for BDS service providers/business advisors wanting to join the RISMEP BDS network. Providers must submit their competency profiles, and complete a written and an oral test to demonstrate their knowledge and performance quality. Once approved as a network member, they are added to the database of BDS service providers along with supporting documentation on their areas of expertise. They are also subjected to follow-up assessment on the quality of services provided to the client. A certification committee, comprised of DIP, the OSMEP, and experts, reviews the applications.

In addition, it could be helpful to encourage the formation of an association of business management consultants in Thailand, which would embrace members of the various business development services provider networks across the country. In Indonesia, not only does the Ministry of Cooperatives and SMEs work collaboratively with the Association of Business Development Services Indonesia (ABDSI) on developing competency standards for BDS providers so as to increase the pool of private sector BDS expertise in the country (Box 3.5), it also recruits members of the ABDSI (qualified consultants and advisors) as part of the referral network of the "Integrated Business Services Centres (PLUT-KUMKM). The formation of an association of business consultants in Thailand would serve to professionalise the market and enlarge the supply of qualified BDS providers to be integrated in the BSDP networks established under the RISMEP mechanism.

Box 3.4. The system of ensuring quality standards of BDS providers in Poland

Description of approach

The Polish Agency for Enterprise Development (PARP) makes use of third-party business support organisations and external consultants to provide BDS to entrepreneurs and SMEs under the national umbrella of the National SME Services Network (KSU). The KSU gathers over 200 member organisations providing state co-financed BDS to SMEs and entrepreneurs, including non-governmental organisations, chambers of commerce and industry, employers' organisations, crafts associations, business incubators, technology centres, credit guarantee funds, and small consulting firms. The cost of the BDS may be partially covered by PARP. PARP is responsible for the functioning of the KSU network, including the accreditation of institutions and consultants, and for providing services to enterprises on the basis of uniform standards, and providing training to KSU consultants to ensure adequate quality of services.

Factors of success

One of the factors behind PARP's success in upgrading the quality and uniformity of standards of publicly-funded BDS in Poland is the method of accreditation of the BDS-providing institutions. All organisations belonging to the KSU network must be an accredited PARP support provider by meeting a certain level of quality standards. This includes having quality management systems compliant with the requirements of the ISO 9001-2001 norm. They must also demonstrate that they have the technical and financial capacities to adequately provide advice, training, and information on financial services to start-ups, micro-enterprises, and SMEs; ensure that services are provided by staff and consultants with the appropriate skills; have a quality assurance system for their services; and act in accordance with professional ethics standards.

Consultants providing business development advice must also be individually accredited by PARP. One of the main criteria is that they have adequate skills and experience in a given area of specialisation in order to be eligible to participate in any PARP-supported consultancy service. Over 1 400 consultants have been accredited to work in the KSU system.

The planning and development of services is supported by a co-ordinating council with representatives from the different types of service providers, including KSU representatives from the regional level, which is an essential feature of the proper functioning of the system. The council meets regularly and helps to generate synergies in the system and increase relevance to needs.

Obstacles and responses

A main obstacle in co-ordinating a network of external BDS providers is ensuring that there are positive evolutions in service offerings and delivery over time, responding to changes in SME needs and improvements in business advice methods. To support this evolution, PARP undertakes research on the demand for and supply of business support services to provide important insights on how to customise services to better meet SMEs' needs, and tests and introduces new services according to defined and monitored standards.

PARP also monitors the activities of business support organisations, including collecting data on the number of clients served, the percentage of start-ups versus existing SMEs supported, and the content of the service provided. This information helps in identifying imbalances in the allocation of services and making necessary adjustments. PARP also undertakes client satisfaction surveys to assess the quality of services provided by the KSU members.

Relevance to Thailand

PARP's role in ensuring the quality of non-governmental and private sector BDS providers in Poland demonstrates the importance of leadership of the BDS system by an SME agency. It offers a potential model for the OSMEP to strengthen the foundational framework for ensuring the quality of BDS provision in Thailand, including through an organised system of accreditation, monitoring, co-ordination and capacity building for BDS provider organisations and consultants undertaken at the central level.

Sources: OECD (2010), Poland Key Issues and Policies, OECD Studies on SMEs and Entrepreneurship, OECD, Paris. Also see Polish Agency for Enterprise Development (PARP), https://en.parp.gov.pl/

Box 3.5. Merits of an association of business consultants in the provision of quality BDS: the case of Indonesia

The Association of Business Development Services Indonesia (ABDSI) formed in 2002 as the outcome of a national conference on business development services. The Association conducts various workshops, seminars and training for SMEs, manages individual professionals who have capacity and competence in business consulting services (accredited "BDS Consultants" complying with competency standards), and provides policy input to the Government.

The ABDSI has become an important partner to the Ministry of Cooperatives and SMEs (MOCSME) in ensuring the delivery of quality BDS to SMEs. In co-operation with the MOCSME, the ABDSI has developed a four-level competency standard for BDS providers (i.e. beginner, intermediate, advanced and master) leading to a national qualification. The competency standard was informed by a review of experiences in other countries and benefited from collaboration with the Ministry of Manpower (responsible for occupational standards). A national curriculum has been developed to enable BDS providers to acquire the national competency standard, which is a requirement for certification as a business advisor. An essential component in the management of the certification programme is the establishment of a national certification body, driven by the ABDSI, which has certified about 1 200 SME advisors through the National Professional Certification Agency.

The ABDSI is also an important partner to the MOCSMEs in implementing the "Integrated Business Services Centres" (PLUT-KUMKM) initiative, which relies heavily on the involvement of private sector organisations with strong BDS expertise. In this regard, the ABDSI provides access to a ready pool of qualified consultants and advisors from among its membership. Branch offices of the ABDSI are also engaged by the MOCSME to provide BDS consultancy to SMEs in areas of the country without a PLUT-KUMKM centre.

The presence of this professional association of business advisors in Indonesia ensures that Government has access to a qualified pool of consultants, allows leveraging of existing private sector expertise for publicly-supported BDS, creates a local demand for BDS, and minimises the negative effects from the possible crowding-out of the private sector consultancy industry. The establishment of a similar association in Thailand could be triggered by co-ordination and start-up support resources by the OSMEP.

Source: OECD (2018b), SME and Entrepreneurship Policy in Indonesia 2018, OECD Studies on SMEs and Entrepreneurship, OECD Publishing, Paris.

Introducing BDS vouchers to create demand for private consultancy services

The wider use of BDS vouchers provided to SME users can also be an important part of the approach to strengthening BDS in Thailand and increasing the use of private sector BDS suppliers. Voucher schemes are commonly used in OECD countries to provide an incentive for SMEs to make use of consultancy from universities, research institutes and private consultancy services. Vouchers are already used by some Thai programmes to incentivise SMEs to secure external consultancy services. Examples are the NSTDA Start-up Voucher and the NIA innovation coupon. The NSTDA does not make use of a list of approved consultants with which the Start-up Voucher must be used; the start-up can engage whichever marketing expert they want for the market expansion project. This could raise quality issues in the delivery of the consultancy service. In the case of the NIA "innovation coupon",[8] the SME is matched with an innovation service provider (ISP) from a private/government educational or research institute that meets certain qualifications and criteria. The NSTDA is advised to follow a similar approach to the NIA by issuing a call for proposals from marketing experts wishing to deliver services under the Start-up Voucher Scheme, perform due diligence on the submitted curriculum vitae, and based on this, establish the list of consultants to be referred to the SME client.

In addition, the OSMEP could design a BDS voucher to match SMEs with appropriate private sector BDS providers. Such a voucher scheme could be enhanced by enabling online matching. For example, the Special Measures to Drive SMEs towards the 4.0 Era included provision for an "expert dispatch" programme, whereby experts would voluntarily register themselves in a designated web-based database to participate in the offer of consultancy services to SMEs. This dispatch mechanism was to encourage members of the network of BDS providers to register with the Ministry of Industry, after meeting certain requirements, and be entitled to place requests for expert dispatch to their client SMEs free of charge (JICA and UNICO International Cooperation, 2018). However, this "dispatch system" was not fully developed and has not been integrated into the SME One portal to facilitate online matching of experts with SMEs' needs. The OSMEP could develop the concept further for implementation.

Expanding online management training

The OSMEP "SME Knowledge Centre" provides e-learning courses for SME managers and owners. Initially under the label of "eSMEs University", the objective is to provide lifelong learning opportunities to all SMEs, many of which may not be able to attend physical training classes due to time, place, work schedules or costs. The e-learning modules are an effective, low-cost, tool for imparting knowledge to a large number of entrepreneurs and SMEs. Attention needs to be paid to disseminating information about these courses to SMEs.

In addition, management training modules formatted for e-learning access could be specifically promoted to SMEs in advanced agriculture and biotechnology and food-for-the-future in Chiang Mai and Chiang Rai. A pilot e-learning approach, tested on SMEs in the Thai food industry cluster to improve their management skills, produced favourable results and demonstrated the potential of this approach for improving accessibility of management training to SMEs (Box 3.6).

Box 3.6. Results from online business management training for SMEs in food clusters in Thailand have been favourable

A web-based management course for SMEs was developed by e-learning professors at the Thai-based Assumption University as a trial to test the appropriateness of an e-learning approach for SMEs in the food industry cluster. The MONARCHIST (Management Obligation and Orientation, Network and Need, Apply, Relation and Recruit, Control, How, Investigate, Satisfied and Training and Treatment) eLearning module in SME Management Skills for Thai Food Industry Clusters was developed on the basis of a learners' needs survey that included in-depth interviews with 30 SMEs in the food industry sector regarding the major problems affecting their management.

The course consisted of nine learning content lessons addressing the priority learning needs of the SMEs, along with practice components and exam testing for each lesson. Some 300 entrepreneurs from the food industry were selected to register for the MONARCHIST training, which they were expected to complete within one month.

Evaluation of the pilot initiative revealed that the post-learning knowledge scores on business management skills were significantly higher than the pre-learning scores, indicating that the SMEs had considerably improved their knowledge and understanding of management skills. The overall learners' satisfaction scores towards the eLearning model were high (4.38 out of 5.00) and shown to be directly related to the course content as well as the system of teaching, graphics and design, lesson components, and internet technical support.

On the basis of the evidence, the researchers concluded that the web-based course was effective and appropriate for implementation. They also suggested that other social media platforms could be used to deploy the e-learning course in addition to more traditional web-based learning models.

Source: Phisarnchananan et al. (2018), "Development of an eLearning Model in SMEs Management Skills for Thai Food Clusters", AU-GSB e-Journal, 11(1), June, Assumption University Press, Thailand, https://pdfs.semanticscholar.org/d628/dde12b1df900183cfdd0c7d2c0660cf5d220.pdf

Creating fast track business development services for the regional innovation cluster

The business development services required for innovative start-ups and scale-ups in strategic sectors for Thailand's future economy need to be more intense and specialised than the basic business advisory support currently aimed at standard SMEs and micro firms. The existing generic support needs to be complemented with an additional set of relatively intense, high-quality and tailored business advice and mentoring services targeted specifically at innovative start-ups and scale-ups, focused on supporting them in integrating innovative products and internationalising markets. Developing this additional "fast track" strand of business development services support is a key challenge and opportunity for clusters like advanced agriculture and biotechnology and food-for-the-future in Chiang Mai and Chiang Rai.

The fast track support should include activities for:

- improving business management capacities impacting on innovation, growth and export performance through inducing changes by managers affecting organisational structures, products and services and production processes;
- facilitating linkages between start-ups and scale-ups and universities and research institutes to assist in testing ideas for new product development and innovation-related projects;

- providing guidance and expertise on marketing strategies and approaches, including packaging and customer targeting; and
- providing technical advice on intellectual property issues, standards and certification.

Key priorities for providing this fast track support in the cluster are set out below.

Including more private consultants in public sector BDS provider networks

As one of the first provinces participating in the RISMEP project, the BDS provider referral network is substantially developed in Chiang Mai province. In addition, the government is starting to build a RISMEP BDS supplier network in Chiang Rai province, having recently signed co-operation agreements with 20 agencies to join the network, including 13 government agencies, two private sector organisations, two academic institutions and three financial institutions.[9]

The RISMEP approach should be continued but with additional efforts to expand the number of private BDS providers connected into the RISMEP-supported system, and its databases and quality standards. Including more private BDS providers in the RISMEP networks could be facilitated by conducting a mapping of private providers in the two provinces, or by issuing a call for private consulting firms and individual consultants to submit applications for inclusion in a common database of qualified BDS providers that could be drawn upon to provide BDS to start-ups and potential scale-ups in the regional innovation cluster.

In addition, potential start-ups and scale-ups in advanced agriculture and biotechnology and food-for-the-future in Chiang Mai and Chiang Rai could benefit greatly from access to the ITAP consultancy services delivered through its networks of technology experts. This includes access to the subsidy to SMEs to cover 50% of the consultancy fees of an appropriate expert, the ITAP "Start-up Voucher", and the IDE4SME Programme problem/needs diagnosis and in-depth consultancy services. At present, it is not obvious that ITAP networks and RISMEP networks are connected or that the consultant databases are integrated. Connecting the ITAP and RISMEP networks would expand the body of expertise that SMEs with innovation potential can access in the cluster, and help to identify more clients with high potential to benefit from ITAP services.

Create cluster management agents to help manage BDS

In addition to issuing a call for private sector BDS suppliers and linking the ITAP and RISMEP BDS supplier lists, the availability of high-quality support for the cluster development can be promoted by allocating resources for a formal dedicated structure to organise BDS for the cluster. The structure would involve a cluster management organisation with cluster management agents undertaking outreach work to identify and target start-ups and scale-ups with innovation and export potential in the cluster. The agents would link the firms to the offer of fast track BDS designed for start-ups and scale-ups in the cluster and provide linkages to support programmes in innovation, training and finance.

Useful guidance for Thailand in a structured approach can be drawn from the United States Small Business Administration's (SBA) Regional Innovation Cluster initiative (see Box 3.7). This aims to supply tailored BDS support to SMEs in regional innovation clusters, packaged with complementary support from the SBA and other federal and state organisations (e.g. innovation, entrepreneurship, capital access, technical assistance, workforce training, export promotion, etc.). As part of the initiative, the SBA identified the specific BDS needs of SMEs in a regional innovation cluster and the related BDS support that should be applied to address these needs (Table 3.1).

Table 3.1. Parameters of business development services in the Small Business Administration Regional Innovation Cluster Initiative, United States of America

Needs of the clusters' small businesses to be addressed in cluster activities*	Six categories of BDS services to be provided in the clusters**
1. Facilitate alliances and collaborations among the cluster participants (targeted networking events, referrals of small businesses to large firms or external network resources, such as universities and research institutes).	1. One-on-one counselling on starting or growing a business: general business consulting, technical assistance, mentoring, business development, international marketing, financing, problem-solving, assisting with the preparation of grant applications for innovation support programmes (e.g. small business R&D or technology transfer programmes).
2. Increase access to capital (e.g. information on financing options, mentoring and assistance in writing applications for various funding opportunities, brokering relationships with financial institutions and venture capitalists).	2. Information dissemination: sharing of relevant information on topics such as supply chain opportunities, industry-relevant reports, location of specialised resources (e.g. prototyping facilities, legal assistance), federal grant and funding programmes, and collaboration opportunities, using a variety of methods (e.g. newsletters, cluster databases/websites, virtual social platforms).
3. Enhance development or commercialisation of new technology (e.g. workshops on technology transfer and commercialisation of new technology, assisting with the various steps involved in developing or commercialising a new product, one-on-one counselling to help in the revision of business strategies to deal with the potential challenges of technology transfer, creating key linkages with universities/research institutes to help in the transfer of new technology or concepts into the marketplace).	3. Training events: group sessions or workshops on topics of interest to the small business cluster participants, such as technology transfer, financing, etc.
4. Improve marketing strategies (e.g. one-on-one counselling and workshops on marketing strategies, facilitating connections with larger organisations to act as mentors, making referrals to other regional resources).	4. Networking events: enabling the small businesses to meet with large businesses, potential contractors, end users of the small businesses' products or services, venture capitalists and investors.
5. Increase exports (e.g. seminars, workshops, individual counselling, referrals to other regional resources specialised in exporting).	5. Matchmaking events: bringing the small businesses together with potential venture partners in particular technology areas.
6. Assist with intellectual property (IP) issues and patent applications (e.g. workshops on IP and how to incorporate IP considerations into business plans and strategies, guidance through the patent application process, facilitating connections with IP specialists to assist with patent applications).	6. Showcasing events: creating opportunities for the small businesses to showcase their technology products or services to potential customers, including demonstrating their prototypes to third parties, pitching competitions, etc.

Source: * Monnard et al. (2014), "The Evaluation of the U.S. Small Business Administration's Regional Innovation Cluster Initiative", Year Three Report. ** Demiralp et al. (2012), "The Evaluation of the U.S. Small Business Administration's Regional Cluster Initiative Year One Report".

Box 3.7. Adapting and co-ordinating BDS for SMEs: the Small Business Administration (SBA) Regional Innovation Clusters initiative, United States of America

Description of the approach

Since 2011, the SBA has supported 14 Regional Innovation Clusters (two related to agricultural technology) to offer co-ordinated and adapted business training, counselling, mentoring, commercialisation and technology transfer services, and other SBA services for the development and growth of small businesses in the clusters. This includes linkages to other federal and state programmes, and notably the Small Business Innovation Research (SBIR) and Small Business Technology Transfer (STTR) programmes. Each cluster received SBA-funding of USD 500 000 for the BDS provision, with a total average annual appropriation since 2014 of about USD 5 million.

Members of these SBA-supported clusters include large firms and small businesses and are firmly embedded in networks of universities/research institutions, business associations, public sector agencies, and non-profit organisations, all crucial participants in an innovation cluster. The SBA-supported clusters could deploy assistance to the small businesses by either providing in-house services, utilising services provided by SBA-affiliated resource partners, such as the Small Business Development Centres (SBDCs), Women's Business Centres (WBCs) and the SCORE programme (consultancy and mentoring services), or leveraging the expertise of third-party resources, such as technical assistance programmes, university business schools and technological institutes. The majority of the clusters selected a mix of these options depending on their local and regional resources and the needs of their small businesses.

Basically, the services and activities provided to small businesses by the clusters can be divided into two broad categories: business services aiming to enhance small businesses' internal capabilities, and events to enhance their external networks. The provision of BDS takes the form of workshops/training sessions involving multiple businesses and one-on-one counselling sessions with individual small businesses. The BDS focuses on a variety of topics, such as business development, intellectual property, exporting/importing, financing, marketing, commercialisation of new technology, partnerships and alliances, and contracting opportunities. The choice of topics depends on the needs and demands of each cluster's small businesses. The networking services materialise through events that provide a platform for small businesses to network with large businesses, other small businesses, and other organisations, including financing entities.

Factors of success

In the first three years of the SBA support, the number of small businesses participating in the clusters increased by 500%; employment in the cluster-supported small businesses grew an average 6.9%, more than four times faster than the regional benchmark; and the revenues of these small businesses also increased by an average 6.9%, almost two times faster than comparable firms (Monnard et al., 2014). During year 3, more than 13 000 hours of one-on-one counselling had been delivered to the small businesses, and 108 training, networking, showcasing and matchmaking events. Sixty percent of the small businesses reported that cluster activity led to the development of new products or services, and one third that it facilitated the commercialisation of new technology. About 75% of the small businesses in the SBA clusters were satisfied with cluster services and activities and 56% reported that the services provided by their clusters were unique and could not have been accessed from other providers outside of the cluster (Monnard et al., 2014). This is a strong indication of the value proposition experienced by the small businesses.

Critical to the success of the SBA RICs was assignment of Cluster Administrators with responsibility for ensuring effective communication between the cluster management team and the small businesses (e.g. monthly networking receptions, bi-monthly update calls on progress, feedback on cluster services, suggestions for events). Close contact with the small businesses and cluster stakeholders improved the capabilities of the cluster team to make referrals, provide tailored assistance, and facilitate the right connections (e.g. collaboration partners, external BDS providers, supply chain linkages).

Obstacles and responses

An initial challenge for the clusters was developing effective outreach strategies to recruit small businesses. The cluster administrators underestimated the importance of cluster promotion and devising a compelling value proposition to attract small businesses. This was overcome by developing formal relationships with chambers of commerce, business associations and other organisations in the innovation and business support ecosystem, developing marketing materials to improve visibility of the cluster, making use of social media, publishing a website (with an open and streamlined online application process), and expanding the number of recruitment channels by leveraging the network of SBA Small Business Offices, and bringing state-based organisations into a formalised governance structure to achieve a stronger cluster identity.

The SBA grant to the cluster could be used for cluster management activity (set-up, strategic planning, co-ordination with regional service providers and partners, cluster promotion, information dissemination) and for service provision (counselling, training, network building). Cluster managers initially underestimated the share of time needed for the small business counselling and mentoring component. To respond to the greater demand for time spent on providing services to the small businesses, the cluster administrators adjusted the percentage of resource allocation between the two activities. In the first year of the SBA initiative, the clusters averaged 39% of their time on cluster management and 61% on providing services to the small businesses (Demiralp et al., 2012). In the third year of the initiative, the clusters were averaging 24% of their time on cluster management, and 76% on providing services to the small businesses (Monnard et al., 2014).

With an increasing number of small businesses attracted as cluster members, cluster administrators were forced to recognise their unique and compelling needs. This required an adjustment in the regular service offerings of the cluster to meet the needs of the small businesses. For example, the cluster managers, used to introducing cluster members to venture capital, realised many small businesses needed a greater understanding of equity capital financing and also linkages to loan options. In response, the cluster administrators provided expert guidance to the small businesses on the advantages of venture capital and how it worked and expanded connections with other financing options, including federal funding programmes. Clusters also hired specialised consultants to offer one-on-one assistance to the small businesses in order to identify federal SBA grants and training and help in identifying and brokering market opportunities with regional supply chain anchor firms.

Relevance for Chiang Mai and Chiang Rai

This initiative provides an example of how a national SME agency can support regional clusters to integrate BDS services into their regular cluster activities. Using this type of approach, the OSMEP could improve the access of existing and potential start-ups and scale-ups with innovation and export potential to BDS and other business support in advanced agriculture and biotechnology and food-for-the-future in Chiang Mai and Chiang Rai. The key feature of the approach is to assign Business Development Advisors to each sub-cluster. They would be responsible for connecting selected start-ups and potential scale-ups to a prescribed menu of counselling, training, networking support and making connections with the range of technology and funding supports available through state and provincial programmes and partner organisations.

Sources of further information: *SBA website: "Innovative Economy Clusters", https://www.sba.gov/content/innovative-economy-clusters; "Regional Clusters Initiative", https://www.sba.gov/sites/default/files/oed_files/Clusters.pdf/. Demiralp et al. (2012), "The Evaluation of the U.S. Small Business Administration's Regional Cluster Initiative Year One Report", Optimal Solutions, Washington, DC. Monnard et al. (2014), "The Evaluation of the U.S. Small Business Administration's Regional Innovation Cluster Initiative Year Three Report", Optimal Solutions Group, Washington, DC.*

Essentially the approach proposed is to adopt a collaborative client-centric service model to BDS provision to start-ups and scale-ups in the cluster based on the cluster management agents identifying and working with individual start-ups and scale-ups with innovation and export potential. The cluster management agent would scout for client firms and assist them in identifying what is needed to strengthen their innovation, growth and export capabilities and develop a plan for moving forward. This would include facilitating linkages with the appropriate public agencies or programmes (e.g. ITAP, NIA, TMC) or resources to provide solutions to those needs, helping the SME implement the plan, and providing ongoing advice and assistance as the SME grows. This would fit within the integrated BDS structure created for the cluster.

It would not be dissimilar to the client-driven approach used in the RISMEP model, whereby:

- RISMEP Facilitators promote and lead the process of developing a co-ordinated services delivery system in the province;
- Co-ordinators plan, arrange and implement support services according to the needs of the individual SME clients; and
- Assistants conduct preliminary interviews with the SMEs before referring them to a counsellor, making use of the Shindan enterprise diagnostic tool to diagnose business needs and determine the most appropriate BDS-provider.

The Innovacorp example from Canada (see Box 3.8 on the provision of BDS to SMEs in an agricultural bioenterprise cluster illustrates how BDS provision can be incorporated in innovation cluster development support through the use of dedicated account managers and access to a network of external consultants and mentors.

Box 3.8. Providing BDS to SMEs in biotechnology clusters, Innovacorp, Nova Scotia, Canada

Description of the approach

Innovacorp is a provincial government body with the mission to foster innovative start-ups in the Nova Scotia region of Canada. In 2014, Innovacorp became the provincial partner in the federal government-supported and funded national Bioenterprise Corporation agri-tech commercialisation accelerator. The Bioenterprise Corporation model consists of assigning a team of analysts and mentors to provide one-on-one mentoring and coaching, business plan support, management team development, technology assessments, marketing strategy direction and other supports to advance innovative agri-food and agri-product technologies. The aim of Innovacorp in this project is helping commercialise Nova Scotia agricultural technologies by providing value added advisory services to high-potential agricultural start-ups and scale-ups, particularly in rural areas.

SMEs in the Nova Scotia bioenterprise cluster include those working on functional foods for human markets, biostimulant fertilizers, use of lipids in biofuels, etc. The Innovacorp model helps client SMEs in the agri-tech cluster find good venture opportunities through the provision of business advisory services and linking them to university researchers to help work on new product development and solutions. Each SME in the cluster is assigned an Innovacorp account manager who helps them innovate with new products and solutions, including setting and meeting growth milestones, and connecting them to a network of external experts to support the firm's advisory and technical needs. Mentoring is facilitated through peer-to-peer opportunities and more formal mentoring engagements with seasoned advisors.

To form the cluster, Innovacorp mapped and categorised all relevant organisations in the ecosystem, including SMEs active in the sector, support entities, research organisations and researchers, and their areas of expertise and scientific competence. It also develops linkages between the cluster members and large companies in the province, and encourages SMEs and new start-ups in the cluster to work with the research community on innovative solutions in response to the needs of the large companies. In effect, the large companies provide a market-pull for innovation in the sector. In 2019, there were 13 agri-tech SMEs in the cluster, geographically located in various parts of the province.

Factors of success

Since the partnership with Bioenterprise Canada began in 2014, Innovacorp has supported more than 63 companies, most of which were start-ups, resulting in 342 jobs and more than CAD 53 million of investment in the sector (Innovacorp, 2019). While the task of identifying the SMEs to participate in the cluster is critical, Innovacorp found it is equally important to integrate researchers early on in the cluster development process as well as to select advisors equipped to work with the SMEs on business models and milestones and to help them to navigate the research milieu.

Assigning an account manager to work with the cluster firms to identify their major problems, answer their compelling questions and plot a path to how these might be addressed is essential, including inviting the research community to develop and test solutions. Also key is the role of the account manager in tapping into the Innovacorp network of (domestic and international) external experts, mentors, specialists and investors to support the cluster SMEs. One of the mentoring strengths is applying the Massachusetts Institute of Technology Venture Mentoring Service model, an approach that uses mentor teams with diverse expertise tailored to the specific needs of each cluster firm (https://vms.mit.edu/mit-venture-mentoring-service).

Obstacles and responses

SMEs in the cluster network require considerable time and attention. Consequently, the account manager for the agri-tech sector spends a considerable amount of time on the telephone with client firms to answer their questions, provide advice, and monitor their progress in meeting set milestones.

Finding competent "lead" account managers to work with the clients can be challenging. Innovacorp seeks to hire people with experience and specialist knowledge and then to invest heavily in training and professional development by, for example, sending the account managers to professional conferences to stay on the leading-edge of cluster support approaches.

Relevance for Chiang Mai and Chiang Rai

The agri-tech bioenterprise cluster example from Canada is akin to the advanced agriculture and biotechnology and food-for-the-future regional innovation cluster in Chiang Mai and Chiang Rai. It illustrates the importance of organising BDS services to SMEs in the cluster by making use of an account manager to serve the needs of individual companies and providing linkages to research institutions, external experts and mentors, and investors to help them access the resources they need to innovate and set and reach established milestones for scaling-up.

Sources of further information: Innovacorp, Halifax, Nova Scotia (https://innovacorp.ca/about); Innovacorp (2019), "Accountability Report 2018-2019", https://innovacorp.ca/sites/default/files/publications/innovacorp_accountability_report_2018_2019.pdf/; About Bioenterprise Corporation – Canada (http://www.bioenterprise.ca).

The OSMEP can take a leadership role in creating these cluster management agents tasked with promoting access to appropriate BDS to promising start-ups and scale-ups in the cluster. The OSMEP has already demonstrated direct experience in support for SMEs participating in local clusters, working in co-ordination with other government ministries and agencies and the non-governmental and private sectors. Some of its activities have focused on what are effectively sub-clusters of a broader regional innovation cluster, including the nascent herb and medical cluster and food and drink cluster in Chiang Rai.

The OSMEP has co-ordinated a number of efforts to boost the capabilities of local SME clusters in traditional sectors. This includes training to cluster SMEs on trade practices and product development, in co-operation with the Federation of Thai Industries (FTI) and the chambers of commerce. The OSMEP has also worked with DIP, the Department of Agriculture Promotion, the Science and Technology Institute of Thailand, and the FTI to develop a SME cluster roadmap and capacity building activities for the clusters in market development, value-added products/packaging, innovation, and marketing techniques.

In 2017, the OSMEP also supported the establishment of five clusters of SMEs, including the Herbal Cluster, where the objective was to promote connectivity among operators, raise their awareness of market demands and boost their capacity to compete at the national and international levels (Box 3.9). By early-2018, the Herbal Cluster included 940 members, composed of growers, herbalists, distributors, and researchers, across nine provinces, including in Chiang Mai. The OSMEP's involvement in this cluster is an excellent example of BDS support to SMEs within a cluster context.

Box 3.9. Example of BDS intervention in the Herbal Cluster

In the Herbal Cluster activity, the OSMEP partnered with the Rajamangala University of Technology, which has a Faculty of Business Administration, a Traditional Medicine College, a Faculty of Science and Technology, academic researchers and eight campuses, to establish and provide the clusters with research knowledge and a range of BDS supports. This included training courses in business planning, marketing strategies, brand building, product development, product packaging, establishing online and offline marketing channels, and enhanced processing techniques. The SMEs were also provided with domestic and international business matching, support in exhibiting their products at trade fairs, and opportunities to develop supply chain linkages with cluster members across the nine provinces.

Source: "The Office of Small and Medium Enterprises Promotion (OSMEP) has Joined Hands with RMUTT to Establish a Network of Herb Clusters in Nine Provinces in Thailand's Four Regions to Boost Economic Growth by at Least 21 Million Baht", Rajamangala University of Technology (RMUTT), 28 February 2018, http://www.eng.rmutt.ac.th/the-office-of-small-and-medium-enterprises-promotion-osmep-has-joined-hands-with-rmutt-to-establish-a-network-of-herb-clusters-in-nine-provinces-in-thailands-four-regions-to-boost-economic/

Building on the RISMEP approach, the OSMEP could also play a leadership role in promoting a collaborative "team-based" approach to improve the elements of BDS delivery to SMEs in advanced agriculture and biotechnology and food-for-the-future. An example of how the integrated approach was applied in the case of a Chiang Mai start-up entrepreneur in the food processing sector is highlighted in Box 3.10.

Box 3.10. An example of the application of the co-ordinated and integrated RISMEP approach to "team consulting"

An entrepreneur in Chiang Mai consulted the IPC RISMEP consultation service counter about starting a business in food processing. After reviewing the needs of the start-up, the entrepreneur was referred to the Chiang Mai Rajabhat University Business Incubator for assistance with sales planning, logo design, and new business registration. In parallel, two independent consultants in the BDS provider network specialised in industrial engineering and production management were referred to help with factory design and registration to the Thai Food and Drug Administration. Specialty expertise from the Mae Jo (agricultural) University Business Incubator in Chiang Mai was brought in to provide assistance with food processing issues, packaging and extension of shelf life. Finally, the Provincial Community Development Office of the Ministry of Interior was able to provide an opportunity for the client to present its products at the exhibition of local specialties. This approach provided "360-support" to the entrepreneur with the various aspects of the start-up process requiring consultancy services.

Source: JICA/UNICO International (2016), "Project for Enhancing Regional Integrated SME Promotion (RISMEP) Mechanism in the Kingdom of Thailand", Project Completion Report (Second phase)", p. 35.

These approaches can be scaled up to the level of the regional advanced agriculture and biotechnology and food-for-the-future cluster as a whole through the development of cluster management agents focused on BDS supply.

There is also scope to co-ordinate the individual level advice for start-ups and scale-ups into support for networks of SMEs, both increasing opportunities for efficiency and for peer learning. Currently, both SMEs requesting assistance and BDS providers register in the online RISMEP system and matches between providers and SMEs are made on an individual basis. This may not be the most appropriate way to meet the more collective needs of SMEs participating in the cluster initiatives. The cluster management agent could be tasked with identifying common BDS needs across potential start-ups and scale-ups in the cluster that could be met by working with groups of SMEs, as opposed to on an individualised basis.

Using vouchers to increase demand for BDS from cluster SMEs

One of the major constraints to developing the innovation capabilities of start-ups and scale-ups through BDS is the reluctance of many SMEs to use these services due to limited awareness of the benefits they can offer, as well as limited knowledge of potential BDS suppliers. Internationally, an increasingly common approach to addressing this problem involves offering SMEs BDS vouchers to be used to obtain subsidised services from accredited BDS suppliers. A BDS voucher for innovative start-ups and scale-ups should be seen as an important part of an effort to integrate BDS into support for advanced agriculture and biotechnology and food-for-the-future development in Chiang Mai and Chiang Rai.

This could complement the generalised BDS voucher scheme recommended above for Thailand as a whole, but offer higher value BDS vouchers for innovation support for SMEs in advanced agriculture and biotechnology and food-for-the-future specifically in Chiang Mai and Chiang Rai. The vouchers would channel these SMEs to high-quality specialised support for the sector in Chiang Mai and Chiang Rai, implemented in concert with a database of approved consultants. In addition, the existing voucher schemes of the NSTDA (Start-up Voucher) and the NIA (Innovation Coupon) could be specifically promoted to start-ups and scale-ups in the regional innovation cluster.

As a potential model, the example in Box 3.11 illustrates the use of a BDS-related voucher scheme by the Danish government to incentivise cluster SMEs to reach out to specialist expertise for help with product development, market development and internationalisation.

Box 3.11. Use of voucher schemes to support SMEs in the BioPeople cluster organisation, Denmark

Description of the approach

BioPeople, the Danish Life Sciences Cluster hosted by the University of Copenhagen, targets companies in the medical industry that are developing equipment, products and services related to biotechnology, biomedicine and pharmaceuticals, as well as companies that research, develop and/or market food ingredients, products and services that have an interface to drugs. The cluster organisation makes use of various voucher schemes to support the knowledge and market access needs of participating SMEs.

BioPeople has been successfully working with innovation vouchers for many years. Small financial incentives between EUR 500 and EUR 7 000 for diverse purposes, such as finding new innovative product or service providers, have helped SMEs generate further growth. Supported by an online database of service providers, the innovation voucher schemes are an important instrument for the cluster organisation to facilitate innovation across industrial sectors.

Diverse vouchers are used as a vehicle to provide practical and financial support to the SMEs involved in its cluster. The BioPeople Boost4Health Voucher programme targets SMEs wishing to explore their international growth potential. It provides for four different-use vouchers, ranging from EUR 500 to EUR 15 000, that can be used for travel to visit experts or attend events abroad (Travel Voucher); to pay for marketing expertise to explore a new international market (Market Expertise Voucher); to cover technical advice, prototyping, demonstration, usability validation or scaling-up (Product Validation Voucher); or obtain advanced consultancy expertise to support internationalisation activity (Impact Voucher).

Factors of success

The voucher schemes have addressed the range of innovation bottlenecks within SMEs, whether these are technological, financial or related to marketing a new product or service in a foreign market. The success of the Boost4Health voucher is further boosted by the offer of tailored coaching to help SMEs meet their immediate business needs and develop future growth plans. The coach guides the SME in defining potential strategies and prioritising actions. Access to a coach means the SME has a regular contact to assist the company. As the strategy develops, the SME is provided with the support needed to ensure its progress, benefiting from the tools and techniques offered by the coach. A key factor in the success of the BioPeople coaching programme is the partnership it has built with Væksthuset (the social enterprise "Greenhouse") to provide the business coaching and arrange workshops on relevant issues (i.e. IP), as well as pitching sessions for the SMEs, which may be tailor-made events or part of a workshop.

Obstacles and responses

Securing funding for voucher schemes can be one of the biggest challenges. The BioPeople cluster had the advantage of being part of an EU-funded initiative to cover costs of the scheme in Denmark. Another challenge can be identifying the list of professional organisations and consultants equipped to provide the services covered by the voucher scheme. Again, BioPeople had the advantage of a ready-made network of service providers/organisations as part of the Northern Europe network of life sciences/biotechnology clusters supported by the EU project. However, making coaches available required identifying a Danish organisation and developing a partnership agreement to provide the coaching services to the cluster's SMEs.

Relevance to Chiang Mai and Chiang Rai

Voucher schemes targeting start-ups and innovative SMEs are already in use in Thailand. However, they tend to be quite tailored in their focus, small in funding scale and not aligned with the cluster initiatives. The OSMEP could broaden the possibilities for integrating BDS services into advanced agriculture and biotechnology and food-for-the-future support in Northern Thailand by designing a voucher scheme to incentivise the SMEs with innovation, growth and export potential to reach out to the business service provider network for counselling, coaching and/or training related to their business development needs. The availability of the BDS voucher scheme would be promoted among the cluster organisations and supported by access to a database of participating BDS providers.

Sources of further information: The BioPeople website: http://www.biopeople.dk; Information on Boost4Health vouchers, https://biopeople.eu/news/show/boost4health-website-is-open-apply-for-vouchers-and-coaching.

Expanding mentoring services

Mentoring is now integrated as a feature of various government programmes in Thailand (e.g. ITAP, Thailand Centre of Excellence for Life Sciences/TCELS, incubators) and its role could be expanded further for start-ups and scale-ups in advanced agriculture and biotechnology and food-for-the-future in Chiang Mai and Chiang Rai.

In expanding the mentoring system, it is important to invest in training of the mentors with the objective of elevating the degree of professionalisation of mentoring practice, with an eventual path towards mentor certification. Support is needed to provide potential mentors with a mentor orientation, covering the role of a mentor, how to be an effective mentor, how to establish a beneficial mentor relationship with the client entrepreneur, what to expect in the mentoring experience, etc. For example, new volunteer mentors in the United States SBA SCORE programme must complete the Mentoring Methodology Training Programme during a 3-month probationary period. During this time, the mentor completes 2-3 online training modules based on five key components to be applied in mentoring sessions, reads and agrees to the standard operating manual and code of ethics, shadows an experienced mentor, and takes part in team mentoring.[10]

Similarly, Enterprise Ireland has taken several steps to ensure the quality of mentoring services by issuing a Conduct and Best Practice Guide (Terms and Conditions) for business mentors. The Guide, provided to new mentors when they join the Enterprise Ireland Mentor Network Panel, sets out the minimum standards for relationship management, intervention approaches, reporting on mentor sessions, and providing feedback on service performance. Mentors can participate in regularly-run mentoring Best Practice Masterclass training events and attend the bi-annual Enterprise Ireland-organised Mentor Networking events to share experiences and knowledge with other mentors on the Mentor Panel.

One step in this direction is the Train the Coach project launched by the OSMEP in partnership with the Institute for SME Development (ISMED) in 2018.[11] The scheme provides potential coaches with access to an online course and will develop a database of coaches with the knowledge, skills and competencies to help SMEs solve their problems. To become certified as a "coach", the applicant must have at least three years of experience in providing advisory services or at least five years of related work experience; complete the online training programme; and have provided advisory services to at least 25 businesses or for at least 100 person-days. The "smecoach.com" website allows SMEs to request a "consultation" and access the database of "coaches". This initiative is well-founded and in line with international practices.

Systematic monitoring should also be instituted during the mentoring assignment. For example, the standard of quality of mentoring services provided through Enterprise Ireland and the LEOs is monitored by requiring mentors to submit reports on the mentoring sessions. The mentored clients are also asked for their feedback on the mentor, the value of the mentoring and level of satisfaction with the mentor service.

Greater use can also be made of virtual mentoring, in line with various successful models internationally. For example, the SBA-supported Service Corps of Retired Executives (SCORE) mentor service in the United States[12] provides mentoring access to start-ups and SMEs through in-person face-to-face sessions or through virtual media (e.g. email, video chat, Google Hangouts, Skype, Facetime).[13] In the case of Ireland, the Enterprise Ireland Mentor Network allows a limited number of Skype interactions per assignment, normally, one or two interactions for a standard 10-visit assignment. While it may be easier to assign a mentor that is geographically closer to the company, a greater emphasis is placed on ensuring the assignment of a mentor with the most relevant industry experience to meet the company's request. In the case of Thailand, a mentoring programme should also consider developing a roster of diaspora mentors who can be called upon to mentor Thai start-ups/growth SMEs using web-based platforms.

Ireland provides an example of how mentoring is integrated in public programmes as a key business development service (Box 3.12).

Box 3.12. Integrating mentoring as a core business development service, Ireland

The Irish Government integrates mentoring services (engaging external mentors) as a key business advisory service and a component of its key public SME and entrepreneurship support programmes, including incubator and growth programmes. The micro and small enterprise clients of the network of Local Enterprise Offices (LEOs) across the regions of Ireland can request a mentor, through an application form, and be approved for 2-3 hours of subsidised mentoring related to a particular issue and up to five mentor assignments in a calendar year. The LEOs may also offer free group mentoring sessions on a scheduled basis for which a number of micro and small enterprises can register.

In addition, Enterprise Ireland (the main public SME agency in Ireland with close hierarchical connections to the LEOs) maintains the Mentor Network Panel, which extends to larger SMEs and those with more growth and export potential that interact directly with the agency, as well as the micro and small enterprise clients of the LEOs. The network consists of more than 400 highly-experienced business people who can be called on to offer practical one-to-one guidance and advice to start-ups and existing SMEs based on their own business experience and relevant to the business needs and goals of the client. Mentors are usually entrepreneurs, company founders, senior executives with international commercial business development experience, etc. The make-up of the mentor panel provides a high degree of diversity of backgrounds and expertise, which is necessary to ensure the differing demands of start-ups, micro-enterprises, and growth-oriented SMEs can be met.

New mentors are recruited into the Mentor Network throughout the year by way of an application and assessment review process. When an Enterprise Ireland client firm applies for specific guidance from a mentor, the Mentor Network team matches the client with a shortlist of mentors who are experienced in the sector or issue. Depending on the client's needs, the client and mentor agree to meet 3, 5, or 10 times (in 1-3-hour sessions) over a period of 3, 6 or 12 months. To cover the costs of the mentorship, the client is offered an Enterprise Ireland grant for up to 10 sessions which Enterprise Ireland pays directly to the mentor; although in some cases, mentors volunteer to advise an Enterprise Ireland client.

A similar mentor network could be set up by the OSMEP in Thailand, focused particularly on start-ups and scale-ups with innovation and export potential.

Source: OECD (2019), SME and Entrepreneurship Policy Ireland, OECD Studies on SMEs and Entrepreneurship, OECD Publishing, Paris.

Greater emphasis should be placed on entrepreneurs as mentors in Thailand. Currently, the mentors are often university professors and lecturers, as opposed to successful business leaders and entrepreneurs. Insights from mentoring programmes in OECD countries reveal that entrepreneurs "who have been there and done that" can be excellent mentors for start-up and growth-potential SMEs if given appropriate training and support.

Monitoring and evaluation of the BDS activities

It is also important to monitor the performance of the proposed BDS structure for the cluster against key objectives (KPIs), including engaging start-ups and scale-ups with innovation and export potential, providing BDS and linking business advice with financial, innovation and other support for SMEs in a cluster.

The USA SBA example outlined in Box 3.7, requires each SBA-supported Regional Innovation Cluster initiative to submit quarterly reports to the SBA on activities and to conduct annual evaluations that consist of surveys of the cluster administrators, the small businesses, and large businesses. The progress monitoring reports present quantitative data on the number of small businesses in the cluster, the types of BDS provided to the small businesses (by percentage), instances of small business collaboration, supply chain integration, commercialisation of a new technology, new products or services, patents, and grants and contracts awarded to small businesses within the cluster. Evaluations of the impact of the BDS activity are based on collecting data on the economic performance of the small businesses in the cluster activities, such as growth in employment, payroll, revenue and sales from exports. This enables the SBA to compare the economic contribution of cluster-supported small businesses relative to regional benchmarks for non-cluster-supported small businesses.

Business incubators

Business incubators can play an important role in regional innovation clusters by increasing the pool of successful start-ups with the capacity to participate in cluster activity (European Commission, 2019). In the case of Chiang Mai and Chiang Rai, incubator programmes can become a feeder system of innovative enterprises in advanced agriculture and biotechnology and food-for-the-future by providing entrepreneurship training, access to research facilities and expertise, linkages with seed capital, and a range of BDS, such as technical assistance and mentoring.

The NSTDA, the Office of Higher Education Commission (OHEC) and the OSMEP all support incubator development in Thailand. One of the main locations for this incubation support is in the universities. Mae Jo University in Chiang Mai, Mae Fah Luang University in Chiang Rai and the branches of the Rajabhat University in Chiang Mai and Chiang Rai all have university incubator programmes supported and subsidised through the Thai University Business Incubators (UBI) programme. In line with international best practices, they offer various forms of BDS as part of their support offer to hosted start-ups. The services include training (including in basic business operation, marketing, accounting and finance, and product/service R&D); coaching and mentoring; and networking with other entrepreneurs and businesses within and outside the incubators (Yamockul et al., 2019). The university business incubators encourage their incubated start-ups to apply university-based research and technologies to develop and/or improve their products and/or services, and have for some time made use of the mentor approach to assist with training and advice.

In addition, the Northern Science Park (NSP) houses a business incubator on the Chiang Mai University campus focused on start-ups in advanced agriculture and biotechnology and food-for-the-future. It offers a well-organised package of BDS-related support including a business diagnostic to evaluate business capability; joint creation of an incubation plan; an Advanced Training Service to enhance business skills, including negotiation, selling, presentation, product positioning, etc.; consulting services from marketing specialists to study product feasibility, financial, tax and legal, costing, and management skills; and business networking to promote public-private partnerships in joint marketing activities, such as exhibitions and trade shows. Each incubating company benefits from four (six-hour) meeting sessions with consultants based on the needs identified in the business diagnosis report, plus access to domestic and international mentors that are identified and selected by the incubator using its own protocol.

The NSP also hosts Northern Innovative Start-up Thailand (NIST), a start-up ecosystem initiative to encourage and support start-up growth led by the Ministry of Science and Technology (MOST), which includes agri-tech and food as one of nine targeted sectors. The selected high-potential start-ups are supported through a six-week Bootcamp, followed by a six-week coaching programme given by leading Thai-based and international experts and entrepreneurs[14] who provide guidance on developing a marketing plan and strategy, accounting and management skills, market research, basic legal concepts, technology matching, and financial and venture analysis.

In addition, the Thai Business Incubator and Science Park Association (THAI-BISPA) operates a national incubator network. This adds value by providing capacity building support and training for business incubator managers and service providers, service standard guidelines, accreditation for business incubator managers, and experience sharing.[15]

Despite these good practices, there is scope to strengthen the delivery of BDS in the university incubators by adopting a more systematised and client-centric approach. This could establish a set schedule of BDS interventions for each incubated start-up. For example, when an enterprise is accepted into an incubator programme, an agreement could be reached to provide a standard and scheduled block of BDS, e.g. a specified number of days of business-related training, workshops, consulting and coaching, and monthly monitoring meetings. In addition, the incubators in Chiang Mai and Chiang Rai should be linked to the BDS-provider networks supported by the RISMEP mechanism, therefore making use of the external consultants and mentors in a government-validated database.

Conclusions and policy recommendations

There is a strong network of public BDS-providing organisations in Chiang Mai and Chiang Rai, as well as networks of external consultants, experts and mentors, and significant BDS provision within a range of innovation, SME support and business incubation programmes. Public entities need to continue to support these information and advisory services to SMEs in general. This overall support framework to SMEs can be strengthened in three main directions – creating an integrated system for referring SMEs to BDS supply, expanding and strengthening the network of private consultants, and expanding on-line management training services for SMEs.

In terms of referring of SMEs to BDS suppliers, the one-stop shops (OSS) system should be maintained. In addition, the public authorities should further develop an integrated SME web portal, thus expanding the reach of physical one-stop shops to a larger number of SMEs, regardless of their location. An online portal can offer "how-to" resources, information on government assistance programmes and suppliers, e-learning courses, and linkages to databases of external BDS providers. The OSMEP has made progress in designing the SME One Portal, however, improvements could be made by linking it to more of the online tools of the OSMEP website, such as the SME Knowledge Centre. In addition, the site could include the shindan enterprise diagnostic tool, which would enable SMEs to self-assess their strengths and weaknesses, identify the key areas they need to work on to improve their performance, and be directed to further support.

A complementary approach would be the provision and promotion of online business management training and resource materials. These would offer SMEs a flexible and online learning environment, taking into consideration the operational and management demands on their time and schedules. This could be within the purview of the OSMEP since it has already supported the development of SME e-University business training modules. The take-up of these modules could be increased through awareness-creating activities by business development advisors.

However, this generic support system, available to all SMEs, is not sufficiently intense, high-quality and specialised to support potential start-ups and scale-ups in advanced agriculture and biotechnology and food-for-the-future in integrating innovation in their products and exporting them. A new fast track strand of BDS support should therefore be developed for the regional innovation cluster, and other regional innovation clusters in Thailand. In developing the fast track, policy should pay attention to making greater use of private sector consultants, developing a cluster management organisation and agents to broker BDS support between suppliers and user firms, delivering BDS support to groups of SMEs, using vouchers to build demand, and expanding mentoring services.

Shifting more BDS from direct public provision to publicly-subsidised private sector provision is in line with the OSMEP's current plans. The public sector would then play more of a brokerage role, rather than direct provision, for the more advanced BDS support for firms in the cluster. The public role would then focus on identifying firms for fast-track support, diagnosing their support needs, linking firms to sources of business development services, incentivising use of business development services with vouchers, and managing performance and quality standards in publicly-subsidised suppliers. A cluster management organisation and cluster development agents could play an important part in such brokerage.

In building this system, it is important to ensure an adequate supply of private consultants/advisors/experts for the fast track system. This requires a mapping exercise of available BDS providers and development of a database of qualified consultants. Actions are also needed to stimulate the demand for private BDS among SMEs. The offer of a subsidised BDS voucher scheme could play this role, incentivising both the demand and the supply of private BDS provision. The RISMEP network could be instrumental in making a database of consultants and mentors available for the purpose of recognising the vouchers in exchange for the service. The business advisors would also follow-up with a schedule of regular meetings to assess the SMEs' progress in meeting milestones.

Mechanisms must also be put in place to monitor and control the quality of BDS provision to SMEs by providers, especially external advisors and consultants who are contracted or subsidised by the government to provide the BDS (e.g. feedback forms from the SME clients; reports from the BDS providers). This is not currently routinely done across agencies and institutions in Thailand. In addition, there may be a need to revert to a more standardised approach to the training, professional development and certification of BDS providers (as in the RISMEP model) that focuses on counselling intervention skills, diagnostic techniques, and practical advice-giving, in addition to knowledge in the functional areas of business.

Actions should be taken in these areas to ensure that BDS is offered alongside of financial and technology support to start-ups and scale-ups in the regional innovation cluster and that oversight responsibility is assigned to a lead organisation. A potential approach would be to assign the roles to an overarching cluster management organisation for advanced agriculture and biotechnology and food-for-the-future in the Chiang Mai and Chiang Rai regions. The cluster management organisation would have cluster management agents with a mandate to ensure that each potential start-up and scale-up in the cluster is referred to the appropriate BDS provider (external advisor, consultant, mentor/coach, or specific technical expert) to address their specific needs

BDS is offered as a component of business incubator programmes in Chiang Mai and Chiang Rai. However, the specifics of the BDS provision is not standardised across the incubator network. This could be enhanced by stating the type of BDS (e.g. individual consulting, mentoring, business management training, etc.) and the number of days of each to be offered as part of the package of incubation services.

Based on this analysis, key recommendations are offered below.

Box 3.13. Recommendations on business development services

Upgrade generic business development services in Thailand

- Maintain the OSMEP One Stop Shops as an entry point for SMEs and entrepreneurs to basic business development information and referral to appropriate BDS providers.
- Enhance the SME One web portal by providing linkages to all relevant government programmes, online business training modules, etc.
- Include the online Shindan diagnostic tool in the SME One web portal and encourage SMEs to use the checklist as a self-assessment of the strengths and weaknesses of their business. Direct SMEs to the SME Knowledge Centre for remedial training and subsidised BDS support, as appropriate.
- Develop and maintain an integrated database of qualified BDS providers, advisors, consultants and mentors available to SMEs according to a standard quality system applying across government entities. The OSMEP, possibly in partnership with the Institute for SME Development (ISMED), should be responsible for registering and certifying publicly-subsidised consultants and developing and supervising standardised training programmes for consultants.
- Actively promote the online business management course models (SME Knowledge Centre) to SMEs, including developing specific modules for advanced agriculture and biotechnology and food-for-the-future firms.

Create a new fast track of business development services in the Chiang Mai and Chiang Rai regional innovation cluster

- Ensure that the networks of BDS-providing organisations and independent consultants are integrated in initiatives that support innovative start-ups and scale-ups in advanced agriculture and biotechnology and food-for-the-future in Chiang Mai and Chiang Rai.
- Connect the Northern Thailand ITAP networks to the RISMEP networks in Chiang Mai and Chiang Rai and ensure that innovative start-ups and scale-ups in advanced agriculture and biotechnology and food-for-the-future have access to the ITAP and IDEA4SME diagnostic and consultancy services, consulting fee subsidies and voucher schemes.
- OSMEP should implement a funding programme to support a strategic offering of high quality and intensive BDS services to existing and potential start-ups and scale-ups with innovation and export potential in advanced agriculture and biotechnology and food-for-the-future in Chiang Mai and Chiang Rai.
- Assign the role of brokering BDS supply and demand to a cluster management organisation for advanced agriculture and biotechnology and food-for-the-future in Chiang Mai and Chiang Rai. The organisation would operate cluster management agents who would identify promising firms to work with and refer them to appropriate suppliers, including through working with existing, smaller cluster organisations.
- Implement a BDS voucher scheme as an incentive for start-ups and scale-ups with potential in advanced agriculture and biotechnology and food-for-the-future activities to seek services from a private BDS provider (following a business diagnostic to identify major areas for improvement of the business).
- Ensure the voucher schemes of the NSTDA and NIA are made available to start-ups and scale-ups with innovation potential in advanced agriculture and biotechnology and food-for-the-future.

- Expand the use of mentor services and broaden the scope of mentors engaged in delivering mentoring to clients by including experienced business leaders and entrepreneurs with a successful track record.
- Monitor and evaluate the performance of the fast-track system against key performance indicators.

Enhance the provision of BDS to incubator clients by specifying the type of BDS (e.g. individual consulting, mentoring, business management training, etc.) and the number of days of each to be offered as part of the standardised packages of incubation services.

References

Committee of Donor Agencies for Small Enterprise Development (2001), *Business Development Services for Small Enterprises: Guiding Principles for Donor Intervention*, World Bank Group, Washington DC, https://www.enterprise-development.org/wp-content/uploads/BDS-Guiding-Principles-2001-English.pdf/

Demiralp, B., M. Turner, and A. Monnard (2012), "The Evaluation of the U.S. Small Business Administration's Regional Cluster Initiative Year One Report", Optimal Solutions Group, College Park, MD, https://www.sba.gov/sites/default/files/aboutsbaarticle/Evaluation_of_the_SBA_Regional_Cluster_Initiative_Year_1_2012_06.pdf

Dong, D.T., and P.T Huyen (2010), "SHINDANSHI: The Japanese Business Management Consultant System", Discussion Paper, No 10 (E), February, Vietnam Development Forum, Hanoi, http://www3.grips.ac.jp/~globalcoe/e/publications/working_papers/polisy/DP10shindanshiE(Feb10).pdf/

Innovacorp (2019), "Accountability Report 2018-2019", Innovacorp, Halifax, Canada, https://innovacorp.ca/sites/default/files/publications/innovacorp_accountability_report_2018_2019.pdf/

JICA/UNICO International Cooperation (2016), "Project for Enhancing Regional Integrated SME Promotion (RISMEP) Mechanism in the Kingdom of Thailand", Project Completion Report (Second phase)", April, Japan International Cooperation Agency (JICA), Tokyo, Japan, http://open_jicareport.jica.go.jp/pdf/12260832_01.pdf/

JICA/UNICO International Cooperation (2018), "Regional Integrated SME Promotion (RISMEP) in the Kingdom of Thailand", Work Completion Report, November, Japan International Cooperation Agency, Tokyo, Japan, http://open_jicareport.jica.go.jp/pdf/12323408.pdf/

Lämmer-Gamp, T., G. Meier zu Köcker, and M. Nerger (2014), Cluster Collaboration and Business Support Tools to Facilitate Entrepreneurship, Crosssectoral Collaboration and Growth, European Cluster Observatory Report, September, European Commission, Brussels, https://ec.europa.eu/docsroom/documents/9972/attachments/1/translations/en/renditions/native/

Monnard, A., L. Leete, and J. Auer (2014), "The Evaluation of the U.S. Small Business Administration's Regional Innovation Cluster Initiative", Year Three Report, Optimal Solutions Group, College Park, MD, https://www.sba.gov/sites/default/files/aboutsbaarticle/SBAClusters_Year3_Report.pdf

OECD (2010), *Poland Key Issues and Policies*, OECD Studies on SMEs and Entrepreneurship, OECD, Paris.

OECD (2017), "Strengthening SME capabilities through a sustainable market for business development services in Belarus", OECD Eurasia Competitiveness Programme, OECD, Paris, https://www.oecd.org/eurasia/competitiveness-programme/eastern-partners/Peer_Review_Note_Business_Development_Services_Belarus.pdf

OECD (2018a), "Leveraging Business Development Services for SME Productivity and Growth: International Experience and Implications for United Kingdom Policy", November, Centre for Entrepreneurship, SMEs, Regions and Cities, OECD, Paris.

OECD (2018b), *SME and Entrepreneurship Policy in Indonesia 2018*, OECD Studies on SMEs and Entrepreneurship, OECD Publishing, Paris.

OECD (2019), *SME and Entrepreneurship Policy in Ireland*, OECD Studies on SMEs and Entrepreneurship, OECD Publishing, Paris, https://doi.org/10.1787/e726f46d-en.

OECD (2020), *International Compendium of Entrepreneurship Policies*, OECD Studies on SMEs and Entrepreneurship, OECD Publishing, Paris, https://doi.org/10.1787/338f1873-en.

Phisarnchananan, P., P. Saengthong, and C. Ketavan (2018), "Development of an eLearning Model in SMEs Management Skills for Thai Food Clusters", *AU-GSB e-Journal*, *11*(1), Assumption University Press, Thailand, https://pdfs.semanticscholar.org/d628/dde12b1df900183cfdd0c7d2c0660cf5d220.pdf/

SBA (Small Business Administration) (2020), "FY 2021 Congressional Justification and FY 2019 Annual Performance Report", U.S. Small Business Administration, Washington, DC, https://www.sba.gov/document/report--congressional-budget-justification-annual-performance-report/

Yamockul, S., R. Pichyangkura, and A. Chandrachai (2019), "University Business Incubators Best Practice: Factors Affecting Thailand UBI Performance", *Academy of Entrepreneurship Journal*, *25*(1).

Notes

[1] "The Ministry of Public Health aims to build a RISMEP mechanism throughout the year 2023", *AEC10News*, 1 October 2019, https://aec10news.com/contents/business/business-movement/37567/. Funding for the expansion and sustainability of RISMEP was sourced from the SME Development Fund under the national Pracha Rat Initiative.

[2] https://oss.sme.go.th/oss/

[3] Described in the OSMEP website at: https://www.sme.go.th/th/cms-detail.php?modulekey=118&id=1384. The programme includes training workshops, in-depth consulting by an on-site consultant, and product and standards analysis, etc. The OSMEP has invited a number of organisations to join the project, such as the Federation of Thai Industries (FTI), the Food Institute, the Institute for Small and Medium Enterprises Development (ISMED), the National Productivity Institute, the Textile Industry Development Institute, the Thai SME Federation Association, and universities, among others.

[4] https://itap.nstda.or.th/th/#what/

[5] The initial Shindan programme, based on the Japanese SME Management Consultants System was introduced in Thailand in 1999 with the objective of developing broad-based diagnostic and counselling skills of Thai business management consultants, leading to certification as "Shindan-Shi". This programme was designed to take 1 044 hours. Over time, it became shortened to 300 hours, and more recently, some organisations hold short "Shindan" courses that take 60 to 70 hours of learners' time to complete, with each course focusing on only one subject area, such as marketing, finance or production, etc. (Dong and Huyen, 2010).

[6] At one point, the OSMEP had considered the establishment of the "Shindan House", an organisation with the responsibility for managing and controlling all activities of the shindan system in Thailand and ensuring the institutionalisation of a standardised approach training and certifying business management consultants (Dong and Huyen, 2010); however, this has not materialised.

[7] RISMEP produced a Compendium of Collaborative Support Models to be used by counsellors at the one-stop service centre consultation counters. This guidance manual also described team formation and roles of team members in responding to the SME client's needs according to their area of specialisation and expertise, and included more than 20 modules dealing with various kinds of counselling and BDS issues.

[8] The NIA concentrates on three core areas of business: Bio-Business, which includes functional foods, food safety solutions, and medical tourism; Eco-Industry, which includes clean industry and eco-products; and Design and Solutions, which includes agri-solutions, logistics, and the biomedical industry.

[9] "Ministry of Agriculture and Agricultural Cooperatives, Chiang Rai Province Organize the MOU of Network of SMEs Support Agencies under the name of 'RISMEP Chiang Rai Province', joining forces with 20 agencies to link various services for entrepreneurs in Chiang Rai province to be able to access", RISMEP news, 23 July 2020, https://rismep.dip.go.th/news/news_detail/73/

[10] https://www.score.org/frequently-asked-questions-about-score/

[11] https://www.thesmecoach.com/

[12] The SCORE Programme of the US-based SBA is an external volunteer network of more than 11 000 business professionals that provides free or low-cost mentoring and training to entrepreneurs in a wide range of settings; donating more than one million hours of online and in-person mentoring, counselling and training time to small businesses nationwide each year (SBA, 2020).

[13] https://www.score.org/find-mentor/

[14] https://nist-nsp.com/project/

[15] https://www.thaibispa.or.th/en/about-us/

4 Foreign direct investment

This chapter examines the potential for inward foreign direct investment (FDI) to stimulate SME participation in the advanced agriculture and biotechnology and food-for-the-future regional innovation cluster in Chiang Mai and Chiang Rai. FDI is likely to be attracted to the cluster in response to growth in its endogenous research, skills and entrepreneurship activity rather than act as the main stimulus for its development. However, there are policy actions that can be undertaken to build the value proposition to incoming FDI, strengthen regional FDI promotion, and develop FDI aftercare and embedding activities. The creation of a cluster management organisation for advanced agriculture and biotechnology and food-for-the-future in Chiang Mai and Chiang Rai could play an important role.

Introduction

Inward Foreign Direct Investment (FDI) activity can play an important role in SME development in regional innovation clusters through local purchasing and technology transfers. However, inward FDI in technology areas such as biotechnology is only attracted when there are strong local assets to exploit, e.g. in the form of capable suppliers, skilled labour, access to research and development (R&D) findings, and social capital. At present, Chiang Mai and Chiang Rai are not attracting substantial inward FDI, but this can change with continued development of the cluster from endogenous sources, particularly as driven by public R&D activities in the region, and with a strengthening of the regional policy arrangements for FDI attraction and embedding.

FDI subsidiaries act as key anchors in regional innovation clusters in many countries, alongside higher education institutions (HEIs) and public research institutions (PRIs). Each of these types of organisations often make contributions to inputting knowledge into SMEs in clusters and connecting cluster SMEs to international markets. Key conditions for contributions of this kind from FDI in the Chiang Mai and Chiang Rai regional innovation cluster are:

- An inward FDI presence in the region with knowledge content in relevant sectors.
- Supply chain and/or innovation collaboration linkages with local actors – including HEIs, research organisations, start-ups and scale-ups.
- Innovation absorption capabilities in start-ups, scale-ups and SMEs, i.e. the quality, efficiency and flexibility to work with FDI and participate in supply chains.

One of the key advantages of FDI for innovation clusters is that they tend to operate with international best practice technologies and this may spill over to SME innovation through a range of channels. The channels may include:

- Demonstration effects – enabling regional SMEs to observe the behaviours of FDI subsidiaries.
- Supply chain upgrading – for example FDI providing engineering support and specialised knowledge to SMEs in their regions.
- Regional labour mobility – whereby FDI managers, engineers and knowledge workers (experts) move between FDI and SMEs or start businesses using best practice methods

On the other hand, there may be also negative impacts from FDI presence in a regional innovation cluster through the accelerated transfer and leakage of useful knowledge and other resources from regional SMEs to the foreign subsidiaries of multinational enterprises (MNEs), rather than vice versa. This has been shown for example in a recent study of high-tech in Finland (Berghall, 2017). SMEs may therefore require advice and support in managing their relationships with inward FDI, particularly around intellectual asset management.

The Chiang Mai and Chiang Rai regions have yet to attract significant FDI in advanced agriculture and biotechnology and food-for-the-future or in other sectors. They are therefore not yet in a position to exploit inward FDI for SME development. The scarce existing FDI does have some local supply chain activities, which could potentially support technology transfer to regional SMEs. However, in general, the FDI operations have arm's length relationships with their local SME suppliers, for example, solely purchasing raw materials in vertical, rather than horizontal, agri-food markets. There are also few linkages between FDI and the universities, science parks, and public research laboratories in Chiang Mai and Chiang Rai and little, if any, research collaboration between inward FDI and domestic SMEs. This is to be expected in that few of the existing FDI operations in Chiang Mai and Chiang Rai are involved in research.

Further, there is an institutional void in Chiang Mai and Chiang Rai for an FDI policy that could attract more investment and integrate it into the regional cluster. There is no regional inward FDI promotion office or economic development agency seeking to attract FDI in target sectors or seeking to build up the Unique Selling Proposition of the region for those target sectors. Nor is there an agency active in FDI aftercare, i.e. supporting existing investors in the region to overcome problems in the region and to reinvest, or in supporting FDI to create local supply and research linkages through matchmaking with regional SMEs and HEIs or reinforcing the capabilities of regional SMEs to supply FDI.

On the other hand, there are a few "green shoots" of FDI that signal the potential for future development in the regional innovation cluster, such as Enza Zaden, a Dutch MNE supporting technology transfer to local agricultural producers (Box 4.1).

Box 4.1. Case study of an FDI operation in Chiang Mai

In 2019, Enza Zaden, a company from the Netherlands, received a BOI promotion in Chiang Mai for its high-tech growing systems. It promotes hydroponics, greenhouses and open field agriculture for vegetables. The company uses technology to produce high-yield, stress- and disease-resistant crops using fewer fertilisers and pesticides. It aims to support local growers in Thailand.

Further information: www.enzazaden.com

The situation in advanced agriculture and biotechnology and food-for-the-future in Chiang Mai and Chiang Mai is therefore that the cluster needs to get established, and this will start to attract more inward FDI, which can then help support the development of supply chains and innovation networks locally.

This indeed is the typical scenario for FDI participation in regional biotechnology clusters. FDI tends to contribute to boosting SME innovation, collaborative network advantage and regional competitiveness in the mature growth stages of biotechnology cluster development, when the clusters are able to attract and embed FDI (Yehoue, 2005; Saha and Fikri, 2014), whereas in the early stages development is driven by research commercialisation from universities and public research through start-ups and scale-ups. For example, technology transfer from FDI was subsidiary to the process of technology generation from knowledge generation institutions in the early days of biotechnology cluster emergence in Silicon Valley (Blakely and Willoughby, 1990). Rather, it was local leading universities and research organisations that generated the relevant technological and organisational knowledge that diffused in innovative SMEs and large firms alike.

In world-leading regional clusters, like Silicon Valley, the pre-existing cluster provides a rich milieu for attracting talent, generating human and social capital, stimulating innovative SMEs with absorptive capacity, and facilitating key employee mobility, which facilitates innovation in emerging technologies and attracts a great deal of private investment, including inward FDI.

The key point for advanced agriculture and biotechnology and food-for-the-future development in Chiang Mai and Chiang Rai is that a policy strategy for technology transfer from FDI needs to be developed in tandem with a policy strategy to support cluster formation processes involving SMEs, rather than as a solution for kick-starting regional cluster development.

The relevance of this approach is supported by evidence from De Propris and Driffield (2006), for example, who show that significant productivity spillovers from inward FDI only occur in mature clusters, and Thompson (2002), who finds that technology transfer from FDI in the garment industry in China has been stronger within clusters than outside of them.

There is also evidence of how FDI has supported SME innovation in established clusters in other middle-income countries. An early example is the Sinos Valley shoe cluster in the State of Rio Grande de Sul in Brazil from 1970 to 1992. The cluster involved 400 local shoe firms in its early stages of development. In later stages these firms were surrounded by many more firms, both domestic and overseas, and the initial cluster was transformed to a dynamic cluster with a total of 1 821 firms in 1991 (Schmitz, 1995). MNEs from the USA and Europe entered the cluster in specialised operations spanning all kinds of value creation services, components and materials in the footwear industry. The FDI brought specialised knowledge flows to SMEs in local service rendering workshops, built the base of trained workers in tanning, leather and footwear machinery occupations, increased demand for specialised SMEs in the rubber industry, and gave SMEs access to international markets via an array of export and forwarding agents. The contribution of FDI was to upgrade and consolidate the design and production of shoes by SMEs in the area, although FDI was not there from the start.

The aim of this chapter is therefore to assess how policy can integrate FDI into the advanced agriculture and biotechnology and food-for-the-future cluster in Chiang Mai and Chiang Rai in the medium term and in this way further support SME innovation in parallel with the measures discussed elsewhere in the report. The chapter proposes two complementary policy solutions:

- *Solution 1: Strengthen FDI policy for advanced agriculture and biotechnology and food-for-the-future in Chiang Mai and Chiang Rai using existing policy structures.*

  Existing agencies responsible for FDI and SME development in Thailand and in Chiang Mai and Chiang Rai may pursue activities to create stronger conditions to attract FDI in advanced agriculture and biotechnology and food-for-the-future. This may include developing more relevant R&D and training in HEIs and the Northern Science Park (NSP); marketing the region and its advantages in the sectors; emphasising the presence of relevant research, graduates and science parks; identifying SMEs with the potential to supply FDI and building their absorptive capacities so that they can participate in supply chains and benefit from knowledge spillovers; and aftercare work with attracted FDI to encourage research and training linkages with regional universities and science parks and supply linkages with regional SMEs.
- *Solution 2: Include FDI engagement activity in the roles of a new Cluster Management Organisation (CMO) for advanced agriculture and biotechnology and food-for-the-future in Chiang Mai and Chiang Rai.*

  The CMO would increase visibility of the advanced agriculture and biotechnology and food-for-the-future innovation activities in Chiang Mai and Chiang Rai to potential inward FDI, create regional networks and trust necessary for collaboration among different stakeholders in the regions, and undertake purposeful brokerage between FDI, SMEs and universities, science parks and incubators in the regions as well as with national and international knowledge transfer intermediaries that can work with Chiang Mai and Chiang Rai enterprises, such as BIOTEC in Bangkok, and beyond in Singapore, Japan, India, etc.

These two policy solutions are complementary and should be pursued together.

Not all regional innovation clusters have a great deal of inward FDI, at least in the early stages of their development, and Chiang Mai and Chiang Rai are not different for the time being. The regional innovation cluster in advanced agriculture and biotechnology and food-for-the-future is in its embryonic stage of international development, in particular in terms of attracting FDI and using it to transfer knowledge to regional SMEs to support their innovation capabilities and access to markets. Both solutions can be adopted and implemented in parallel for building the future FDI role in the cluster.

The rest of this chapter discusses this agenda. Section two presents Thailand's FDI performance and FDI policy arrangements. Sections three and four respectively describe the two complementary policy solutions proposed to building the contribution of FDI to SME development in advanced agriculture and biotechnology and food-for-the-future in Chiang Mai and Chiang Rai. Section five provides summary conclusions and policy recommendations.

Foreign direct investment performance and policy arrangements

Thailand has experienced large fluctuations in the value of its inflows of FDI in the past two decades, but overall inward FDI to Thailand has been low compared with South East Asia as a whole (Table 4.1). The composition of this inward FDI includes significant inflows from Asia, led by investors from Japan, China and Singapore, and significant reinvestment by MNEs already present in the country.

Table 4.1. FDI inflows

	FDI inflows in USD millions					FDI inflows as % of gross domestic fixed capital formation			
	2005-07	**2015**	**2016**	**2017**	**2018**	**2005-07**	**2016**	**2017**	**2018**
Thailand	8 451	5 624	1 815	6 478	10 493	14.2	1.9	6.1	9.4
Malaysia	6 240	10 082	11 336	9 399	8 091	16.4	14.8	11.8	9.4
Indonesia	6 726	16 641	3 921	20 579	21 980	6.1	1.3	6.3	6.7
South East Asia	61 712	114 276	116 768	144 177	148 694	20.6	16.2	18.8	18.6
Asia & Oceania	291 439	516 028	474 458	493 782	513 420	10.7	6.1	5.9	5.7
Developing Economies	419 126	728 814	656 290	690 576	706 043	11.5	7.2	7.0	6.8
World (billions)	1 414	2 038	1 918	1 497	1 297	11.4	10.2	7.5	6.0

Source: World Investment Report 2019, UNCTAD

Data from Thailand's Board of Investments (BOI) shows approvals for BOI privileges available in certain geographic areas and industrial sectors in the country broken down by firm ownership (100% Thai, Foreign owned, or joint venture). Table 4.2 shows the breakdown of approvals from 2016-2018 for Northern Thailand as a whole. A substantial share of these projects are in Chiang Mai and Chiang Rai provinces (Table 4.3).

Table 4.2. Board of Investment (BOI) investment incentive approvals by investor origin, Northern Region, Thailand

	2016		2017		2018	
Investor origin	No. projects	Capital investment (THB million)	No. projects	Capital investment (THB million)	No. projects	Capital investment (THB million)
Thai investment	106	10 909	47	3 915	20	2 223
Foreign direct investment	33	6 351	36	8 743	32	4 548
Joint venture	11	755	5	259	12	248
Total	150	18 015	88	12 917	64	7 019

*Note:*BOI applications are made for the purposes of receiving BOI privileges in a certain geographic areas and certain industrial sectors.
Source: Board of Investment Thailand, https://chiangmai.boi.go.th/index.php/investment_file_download

Table 4.3. BOI investment incentive approvals in Chiang Mai and Chiang Rai

Province	2016		2017		2018	
	No. projects	Capital investment (THB million)	No. projects	Capital investment (THB million)	No. projects	Capital investment (THB million)
Chiang Mai	82	2 713	31	6 007	33	2 798
Chiang Rai	5	1 290	7	324	7	249
Total	87	4 003	38	6 331	40	3 047

Source: Board of Investment Thailand, https://chiangmai.boi.go.th/index.php/invesment_file_download

Table 4.4 shows the distribution of BOI incentive approvals by sector. Chiang Mai saw the largest investment, followed by Lamphun, Chiang Rai and Khamphaengphet. Overall, one-third of the approved investment projects were from FDI, ranging from 88% in Chiang Mai to 12% in Chiang Rai.

Table 4.4. BOI investment incentive approvals by industry in the Northern Region

Industry	2016		2017		2018	
	No. projects	Capital investment (THB million)	No. projects	Capital investment (THB million)	No. projects	Capital investment (THB million)
Agriculture and agricultural products	41	17 037	21	1 870	12	1 715
Mining, ceramics and basic metals	5	284	0	0	2	342
Light industry	8	4 573	6	214	5	705
Metal products, machinery and transport equipment	7	1 334	4	406	3	560
Electronic industry and electric appliances	24	2 261	45	3 231	6	491
Chemicals, paper and plastics	11	4 345	0	0	0	0
Services and public utilities	19	4 661	17	5 578	17	2 993
Total	115	34 495	93	11 299	45	6 806

Source: Board of Investment Thailand, https://chiangmai.boi.go.th/index.php/invesment_file_download

Overall, the long-term, inward FDI performance of Thailand is rather weak and needs to be strengthened with appropriate policy actions. In terms of regulations, Thailand ranks relatively well internationally, in 21st position in the World Bank's Ease of Doing Business Indicators 2020, although there should be improvements to the intellectual property system to encourage foreign companies to bring the latest technologies to Thailand.

However, some of the important FDI attraction and aftercare activities that would promote greater FDI inflows are missing or patchy in Thailand at the regional level. Straightforward actions like promoting financial incentives for Industry 4.0, information sharing webinars with government officials and business leaders including showcasing MNEs and SMEs, open access databases and the like are missing in the BOI case. The activities of the Malaysian Investment Development Authority (Malaysia's Investment Promotion Agency) offer a potential model for a more comprehensive system of financial incentives and information sharing activities.

The two sets of policy actions discussed below can help increase the role of inward FDI in promoting SME development in the advanced agriculture and biotechnology and food-for-the-future sectors in Chiang Mai and Chai Rai. Both of these actions can be pursued together. If a CMO is created it can undertake some of the activities related to strengthening FDI policy in the regional innovation cluster, but others concern mainly different actors.

Strengthening foreign direct investment policy in the regional innovation cluster

The FDI policies of many countries include a strong focus on attracting FDI to regional clusters, where the country has the strongest value propositions for investors in particular sectors. This includes the FDI marketing activities of the Investment Promotion Agencies (IPAs), public investments in building sector-relevant infrastructures and skills as well as activities to build FDI supply chains in regional clusters. This is not currently a strong feature of FDI policy in Thailand.

An initial step would be for the BOI, as the Investment Promotion Agency, to include cluster promotion as one of the core elements of its mission. This would include more systematic FDI attraction, aftercare and embedding strategies for regional innovation clusters in Thailand in general, undertaken in co-operation with national research agencies, the OSMEP for the promotion of SMEs, and university science parks, such as the NSP. It would include an explicit focus on the advanced agriculture and biotechnology and food-for-the-future sectors in Chiang Mai and Chiang Rai.

The BOI could undertake the following specific activities for the regional clusters:

1. Sharing data about stocks and inflows of FDI, including information on BOI incentive applications and projects by sector, size and cluster. For the time being, relevant government FDI data is collected and kept across several departments without a single point of contact. This makes it difficult to organise support from related agencies for FDI attraction, aftercare and embedding initiatives in regional innovation clusters.
2. Marketing the strengths of the regional innovation clusters to potential inward FDI, including, for example, the top-10 reasons for FDI in specific sectors to choose a specific regional innovation cluster location within Thailand.
3. Carrying out FDI aftercare at the regional level, including through co-operation with other agencies in regional innovation clusters.
4. Co-operating with other agencies in regional innovation clusters to support the embedding of inward FDI. This should involve connections with the OSMEP, science parks, the Federation of Thai Industry and other regional bodies in order to broker connections between FDI and potential SME suppliers in clusters. It should include supplier development initiatives to support potential SMEs to reach necessary standards of quality, efficiency and price, and flexibility to be successful in gaining supply contracts with FDI.

The relative emphasis at the outset will be on increasing the international marketing of regional innovation clusters to potential inward FDI. As the stock of FDI in regional clusters grows, the scale of the FDI aftercare and FDI-SME linkage building activities will need to grow.

The advanced agriculture and biotechnology and food-for-the-future regional innovation cluster in Chiang Mai and Chiang Rai can serve as a pilot for reinforced FDI activities for other regional innovation clusters in Thailand. The following specific actions could form the basis of the regional pilot exercise:

1. Formation of an FDI-SME linkage strategy team in Chiang Mai and Chiang Rai with adequate skills and resources from BOI, the OSMEP and NSP. This team would develop and co-ordinate the actions with foreign investors.
2. Gathering and presenting data on the cluster with respect to attracting FDI and creating linkages with SMEs. This would require research, secondary data collection, and meetings with local stakeholders. The information should cover topics related to the attractiveness of the region to

FDI in the specific sectors, such as skills availability, research strengths and SME supply capabilities of the cluster. This should feed into marketing communications on the cluster to potential inward FDI. The information should also identify the potential of specific SMEs in Chiang Mai and Chiang Rai for supplying specific FDI operations and the finance and other support needs for these SMEs to reach the capability level required to supply FDI.

3. Developmental actions which keep up the impetus of the linkage strategy team, identifying future opportunities and maintaining the engagement of both FDI and SME sectors. The actions include formalising networking and contacts with FDI. In addition, actions may include development of a transparent system via the NSP and the OSMEP to give comprehensive support to potential SME suppliers including technology development, business development services and development finance, developing the research base, developing more flexible skills, and promoting entrepreneurship in the cluster.
4. A set of remedial actions relating to national regulatory barriers, such as in the area of regulations for operating FDI projects or developing land for FDI projects, which can be mitigated by local actions.
5. A small set of pilot actions designed to create some initial FDI-SME supply linkages or FDI participation in regional research or entrepreneurship development projects with one or more initial FDI ventures. The aim of the pilot actions is to create networking between FDI and SMEs and research organisations, demonstrate the requirements and engagement models of foreign investors to SMEs and research organisations, and give experience to the linkage strategy team.

The OSMEP has an important potential role to play in this agenda by supporting the identification of SMEs that are potential suppliers to FDI, introducing these SMEs to FDI, and strengthening their capabilities to act as suppliers to FDI ventures through business advice and financial support. However, the development of an FDI strategy for the regional innovation cluster, from FDI attraction, to aftercare, to embedding will require a partnership across a range of government departments with responsibilities in this field, including the BOI and the OSMEP, but also government departments such as the Department of Intellectual Property, the Department of Business Development, and the Department of International Trade Promotion.

In addition, the locations and sectors in which fiscal incentives for investment are offered should be reviewed with a view to increasing the attractiveness of regional innovation clusters to FDI. Fiscal incentives that are highly relevant for FDI attraction are currently available in Special Economic Zones (SEZs) and the Eastern Corridor, including incentives focused on the NSP. Consideration should be given to focusing incentives on the regions that dominate Thailand's priority sectors for driving future innovation-based growth, including advanced agriculture and biotechnology and food-for-the-future in Chiang Mai and Chiang Rai, on a similar model to the existing Eastern Corridor.

Foreign direct investment engagement by a new cluster management organisation

This section proposes the inclusion of FDI-SME linkage building activities in the remit of a cluster management organisation for advanced agriculture and biotechnology and food-for-the-future in Chiang Mai and Chiang Rai. If such an CMO is created and takes on FDI functions as part of its activities, it could be involved in some of the activities related to strengthening FDI policy in the regional innovation cluster mentioned above, namely sharing data about FDI in the cluster, carrying out FDI aftercare activity for the cluster, brokering connections between FDI and potential suppliers in clusters, and undertaking potential FDI-SME linkage building pilot actions for the cluster. The specific FDI engagement activities proposed for the CMO are set out further below.

Why a Cluster Management Organisation?

The Cluster Management Organisation (CMO) is a commonly-used innovation policy tool in OECD and other innovation-based economies. Their main function is to strengthen connectivity within the regional innovation clusters they serve. They do this through developing networks, collaborations, and shared visions in a range of key areas for cluster development including skills development, R&D projects, supplier development, and increasing the visibility and attractiveness of a cluster. Connectivity drives innovation performance and competitiveness, and this cannot be simply left to accident and serendipity.

An important distinction can be made between two types of knowledge production in innovation systems (Nowotny et al, 2003):

- **Mode 1:** Knowledge production motivated by "basic research" and disciplinary-based scientific inquiry that it is not primarily concerned by the applicability of its findings. Mode 1 is founded on a conceptualisation of science as separated into discrete academic disciplines, for example, a biologist carries out only biological research and not chemistry research.
- **Mode 2:** Knowledge production by multidisciplinary teams brought together for short periods of time to work on specific, real world problems in collaborative applied research projects. Mode 2 advances the knowledge of the cluster and builds up the innovation absorptive capacities of the SMEs and other stakeholders.

The CMO approach will contribute to Mode 2 knowledge production in the advanced agriculture and biotechnology and food-for-the-future cluster in Chiang Mai and Chiang Rai. This is particularly appropriate to the assets and challenges of the regions in exploiting knowledge generated and transferred by the region's young universities and its science parks. It emphasises cross-fertilisation of knowledge and enabling the growth of start-ups, scale ups and innovative SMEs.

Mode 2 knowledge production can be promoted in the cluster through public sector part-funding of collaborative R&D projects via the CMO (in Minalogic – see Box 4.2 – the typical public sector contribution is 50% of project R&D costs covered by the state and 50% covered by private companies). Scientists in the regional public research organisations and university science parks can be funded as part of collaborative projects for upgrading advanced agriculture and biotechnology and food-for-the-future knowledge generation and transfer on the basis of five principles: knowledge produced in the context of application; transdisciplinarity; heterogeneity and organizational diversity; social accountability and reflexivity; and quality control.

Inward FDI can be involved in these processes as it is attracted to Chiang Mai and Chiang Rai, on condition of gradually building up a culture of collaborative research in Mode 2. Barriers that need to be addressed are that the MNEs in the regions are rare and have so far shown very little, if any interest, in collaborative research with SMEs and universities and science parks. Furthermore, when MNEs show an interest in SMEs, it would be as a prelude for an acquisition rather than fostering knowledge flows through collaborative projects. Furthermore, SME owners still tend to feel that they should be 100% funded by the government for undertaking research.

The CMO can address these issues by working to attract FDI and fostering collaboration and networking among MNEs, SMEs, science parks and government agencies in R&D, supplier development and skills development activities.

There are various examples internationally of public programmes supporting CMOs that promote FDI participation in cluster research, skills and supply networks. An example is the Danish Networking (Brokering) Programme, which was designed by the Danish Technological Institute, funded by the central government and implemented by the National Agency for Industry and Trade (NAIT). The NAIT was the trusted broker that strengthened co-operation and identified opportunities for regional SMEs to benefit from R&D collaboration with inward FDI. Over the 5-year implementation period of the programme in Denmark as a whole, 5 000 firms collaborated and formed networks out of a target group of approximately 12 000 enterprises (Yehoue, 2005, 21).

Similarly, CMOs have been a key tool for innovation and entrepreneurship policy in France. Professional CMO managers and agents have been engaged to connect regional SMEs with large focal firms (both large domestic and foreign-owned firms) within clusters via collaborative projects supported by the French government through the 'poles de competitivité' programme. Lefebvre (2013) argues that these CMOs led to a shift from accidental to purposeful cluster brokerage in the clusters. An example is the micro-nano technologies cluster in Grenoble, France, where a CMO has created strong connectivity among large public research laboratories (similar to BIOTEC in Thailand) and universities, research-intensive large firms including FDI, and an array of SMEs (see Box 4.2).

Box 4.2. The Minalogic CMO, Grenoble, France

Description of the approach

Minalogic is a regional innovation cluster ("*pôle de competitivité*") focused on digital technologies in micro-electronics and nano-technologies (including embedded software and services such as the cloud and 5G innovations). It is located in Grenoble in the Auvergne Rhone Alpes region of France. Minalogic operates through a CMO, which is hosted in MINATEC, part of the public research laboratory for miniaturisation technologies of the French atomic energy organisation (CEA LETI: http://www.leti-cea.com/cea-tech/leti/english). CEA LETI specialises in the emerging alternative forms of "green" energy and ICT Key Enabling Technologies (KETs).

Grenoble is considered as the Silicon Valley of Europe; ranked by Forbes magazine in 2013 as the 5th most innovative city in the world based on the number of patents per 10 000 citizens, and with a long history of cluster development and FDI attraction in micro-electronics and nano-technologies. The cluster includes an anchor firm, ST Micro-electronics, the largest European integrated semiconductor firm, founded by an international French-Italian-Swiss joint venture. It hosts the largest concentration of researchers and public research laboratories in France outside Paris. It includes unique large infrastructures at the European Union level, such as the European Synchrotron Radiation Facility and the European Molecular Biology Laboratory. It also hosts the European R&D headquarters of major USA-based MNEs such as Hewlett Packard and Xerox and industry associations such as SEMI (an association for semiconductors in Silicon Valley, California, and worldwide).

The CMO of Minalogic is a government agency in itself, supported by the local, regional and national governments with an annual budget of EUR 1-2 million. It is locally rooted (and globally connected) with about 20 permanent staff (experts from technical fields to business development and SME promotion) and currently maintains regional offices, not only in Grenoble, but also in Lyon and Saint Etienne, the other main cities of the Auvergne Rhone Alpes region.

The CMO plays a number of pivotal roles in the development of the regional innovation cluster and in supporting FDI-SME linkages:

- Steering public and private research spending towards producing innovations for application in new products and services in KETs in micro- and nano-electronics, photonics and embedded software technology, in application areas ranging from ICT and healthcare, to energy and construction, sport, and advanced manufacturing, including applications for the defence sector. It does this by feeding R&D collaboration proposals from regional actors to selection panels of technical experts and government representatives at different levels for potential funding, based on their commercialisation potential.

- Raising the profile of the cluster at national and international scales, for example, by connecting with the "Silicon Europe" project and the Dresden micro-electronics cluster led by large German MNEs, which helps in the attraction of FDI.
- Brokering R&D collaborations among regional actors, including making connections for innovative SMEs to FDI and research organisations, through putting together and funding large research projects.

Minalogic is supported by generous public research funding for collaborative R&D projects (a total of EUR 881 million from French government research programmes since its establishment from 2005-2019). It nurtures hundreds of public-private collaborative research projects on a competitive basis, funded 50:50 by industry and government. As of 2019, 586 projects had been funded through Minalogic, involving more than 350 small and large companies, plus universities and public research labs in the city-region.

The French government has also created a dedicated inward FDI agency (AEPI – *Agence des études pour la promotion de l'Isère*) to promote inward FDI to the Minalogic cluster and more broadly to attract and embed FDI to the region. In the last decade or so, it has attracted leading FDI projects including from ARM, UK (now in Japanese ownership), GE Healthcare (with respect to med-tech operations), and Rolls Royce (with respect to cleantech). Each has opened offices near Minalogic so that they are in a good physical location to join in with applications for collaborative R&D projects with regional SMEs and research organisations (CEA-LETI and others).

The activities of the CMO have had positive results in stimulating knowledge flows, commercialisation of new products and services, attracting internationally mobile highly skilled labour particularly the "new Argonaut" returnees from world-leading clusters (e.g. Silicon Valley, United States and clusters in Israel), facilitating inward FDI and enabling public-private partnerships.

Factors of success

The Minalogic CMO has the benefit of being located in a very dense and sophisticated regional innovation system with substantial R&D activity, skills generation, and business activity. It therefore builds on a high level of pre-existing high-tech cluster activities and a very supportive innovative milieu and institutional environment in Grenoble (Assimakopoulos et al 2021 forthcoming).

In this context, the CMO has played a critical role in building R&D connections among the regional cluster actors and linking FDI and SMEs. It puts a premium on frequent individual meetings with regional cluster actors to discuss project opportunities and potential connections with other firms and organisations.

Having an active team and management that mixes skills and profiles from the private and research sectors has been important to the credibility of the CMO with local actors and hence its effectiveness. As an independent actor, it has been able to foster trust among the local actors.

The potential access to R&D project funding has incentivised participation by all the actors in the joint activities, which has helped build new areas of collaboration. The competitive nature of the R&D grants has been a tool to steer the collaborations towards promising new areas of exploitation.

A further key to success has been opening up the long standing research and infrastructure of the public research laboratories, like CEA LETI, and capitalising on the knowledge and infrastructure of the European Synchrotron Radiation Facility, the European Molecular Biology Laboratory and the University Grenoble Alpes to collaboration with industry through government funding to collaborative research projects.

Obstacles and responses

In the early stages of the activities of the CMO there was relatively little involvement of SMEs (Potter, 2009). The key players in designing the cluster vision and in R&D collaborations were the large firms and the research institutions. However, a shift was made in the 2010s to give an explicit priority to the CMO on involving innovative SMEs as CMO members and to give an advantage in R&D project bidding to projects involving innovative SMEs. An example is the involvement of Presto Engineering, founded by a returnee from Silicon Valley (Assimakopoulos et al 2016).

Relevance to Chiang Mai and Chiang Rai

Creation of a CMO would help to fill the institutional void in Chiang Mai and Chiang Rai for an overall region-level player brokering connections across all the actors – FDI, SMEs, science parks, research organisations, universities, government departments and agencies.

It illustrates a way of steering research funding to universities and research organisations towards potential commercial outcomes by making funding competitive and conditional on collaborations with firms. It also shows the importance of a team of people who meet with FDI ventures, local SMEs and research organisations to promote research.

Whereas the key research actors and infrastructures of Minalogic are within the region, a CMO for advanced agriculture and biotechnology and food-for-the-future in Chiang Mai and Chiang Rai would also involve collaborations with the BIOTEC national research laboratory in the Bangkok area. Also, whereas the CMO in Grenoble is hosted in a major public research laboratory, the management and team could be hosted in the NSP or the FTI regional office in Chiang Mai and Chiang Rai.

It is also important that a CMO in Chiang Mai and Chiang Rai includes a dedicated FDI team, including support from the BOI, to foster FDI attraction. This work is done in Grenoble by AEPI working in collaboration with the CMO.

Clearly, whereas the focus of FDI attraction in Grenoble has been electronics investments from the United States, Germany and the UK in particular, the focus for FDI attraction for Chiang Mai and Chiang Rai will be in advanced agriculture and biotechnology and food-for-the-future. It would seek incoming FDI activities with knowledge and research content and potential linkages with regional SMEs and research organisations, and target countries such as Singapore and Japan, and to a lesser extent China and India, among others.

Sources of further information: https://www.minalogic.com/en/home. Assimakopoulos, D., M. Tsouri, D. Mavridis, and A. Moore (2016), "Don't lose sight of the forest for the trees: Minalogic and Presto Engineering as a 'New Argonaut' in a French ICT ecosystem", in Wang, H. and Y. Liu (eds), Entrepreneur and Talent Management from a Global Perspective: Global Returnees, Edward Elgar, Cheltenham: 251-272.
Assimakopoulos, D., H. Lawton Smith, N. Baines, M. Tsouri, and S. Romeo (forthcoming), "Oxford and Grenoble: knowledge organisations in local development revisited", Regional Studies, October 1 2021.
Potter, J. (2009), "The micro-nanotechnology cluster of Grenoble, France", in J. Potter and G. Miranda (eds), Clusters, Innovation and Entrepreneurship, OECD Publications, Paris.

The activities that CMOs play in leading OECD country clusters for FDI attraction and embedding, as well as generating other connections, are clearly missing in the case of advanced agriculture and biotechnology and food-for-the-future in Chiang Mai and Chiang Rai.

Broad domains of foreign direct investment policy activity for a CMO

A CMO for advanced agriculture and biotechnology and food-for-the-future in Chiang Mai and Chiang Rai can play important roles in a number of broad domains of FDI activity:

- Increasing the visibility of the regions to potential incoming FDI by helping prepare information on their strengths for marketing materials (highlighting in particular the research and skills outputs of the regional universities – e.g. the medical school, pharmacology department, and department for cosmetic science and biodiversity protection – and the NSP) and making contacts on the ground for potential inward investors.
- Helping identify research collaboration opportunities for FDI with universities, science parks and research organisations in the cluster.
- Helping integrate FDI into supportive supply chains with SMEs.
- Involving FDI in supporting entrepreneurship, for example encouraging FDI operations to work with business angel networks and venture capitalists in improving access to financing and linking FDI with business incubators to provide mentoring and financing and other support.
- Helping steer national-level skills development towards the needs of incoming FDI, including steering the content of continuous education programmes and specialised professional Masters programmes (e.g. MBAs and Masters in a variety of disciplines from engineering to pharmacology to management, finance, marketing and accounting).

Foreign direct investment engagement actions of the cluster management organisation in the cluster

The CMO would undertake the following main actions with respect to FDI engagement activity aimed at SME development within the cluster:

1. Identifying FDI projects already hosted in Chiang Mai and Chiang Rai with cluster-related activities and establishing regular contacts with them. As part of this relationship building, support FDI to overcome any operational problems locally, for example with regulations, and promote reinvestment and contributions to regional cluster development.
2. Identifying the critical mass of SMEs with capabilities in advanced agriculture and biotechnology and food-for-the-future, including a complete directory and a mapping exercise. This could be co-ordinated by the CMO and undertaken by the NSP in conjunction with the Federation of Thai Industries. The output could be used to help build the marketing of the cluster to FDI.
3. Selecting the most capable SMEs from the mapping exercise for support with a view to connect them with inward FDI in supplier chain initiatives. This could be facilitated by one-stop shop consultants working for the OSMEP. The support could involve an integrated package of consultancy, finance, training and innovation support to develop technical and management skills in high potential SMEs in order to build their capabilities for engagement with FDI.
4. Brokering and nurturing SME supply chains with FDI operations. Arrangements can be brokered, for example, whereby an FDI takes equity in an SME in exchange for making investment in new product development in the SME.
5. Encouraging collaborative R&D projects between FDI, SMEs, universities, science parks including NSP, NSTDA and BIOTEC and others. This could involve financial incentives to participate in collaborative R&D projects as an incentive to get involved in applied research and its commercialisation and to build a culture of trust and collaboration amongst the players.
6. Encouraging the role of FDI in corporate entrepreneurship and promoting serial entrepreneurs in the regions, addressing the lack of existing resources in terms of knowledge and finance (private innovation support mechanisms have to be combined with public support mechanisms).

Making links with foreign direct investment in other clusters internationally

There is also potential for the CMO to connect SMEs to MNEs in related clusters outside of Thailand to promote international supply opportunities, for example on product testing. This could be achieved by the CMO in Chiang Mai and Chiang Rai making links with other advanced agriculture and biotechnology and food-for-the-future clusters internationally. These co-operations among related CMOs would aim to broker cross-national FDI-SME linkages and could also extend to other collaborations such as research collaboration. An example of a related CMO with which linkages could be made is given in Box 4.3.

Box 4.3. The Cosmetic Valley CMO, France

The CMO of Cosmetic Valley is based in the city of Chartres, France (about 100 km west of Paris). Cluster policy in France differentiates between "national" and "global" competitiveness clusters. As a national cluster, the Cosmetic Valley CMO receives a much smaller government budget and employs about half of the staff of the Minalogic cluster in Grenoble (Box 4.2), which is in the category of global clusters. Furthermore, Cosmetic Valley covers all the French regions (but with a main focus in the North of the country). Hence, it is not a geographically-agglomerated cluster like Minalogic but a distributed cluster organisation.

As well as maintaining connections with national players and FDI hosted in France, the CMO maintains links with other cosmetic clusters internationally, particularly in Italy and the European Union, but also further afield. Specialised service providers participate in the regional linkage strategy and provide connectivity for SMEs in the Cosmetic Valley cluster with partners internationally. For example, the SpinControl Group (https://spincontrolgroup.com/spincontrol-around-world/thailand) specialises in the scientific substantiation of aesthetical and well-being claims for cosmetics, food supplements, and medical devices. For this purpose it carries out new product testing in global locations, and maintains linkages with Thailand through its Asian office in Bangkok.

The opportunity for Chiang Mai and Chiang Rai is to connect with CMOs in other countries, such as Cosmetic Valley in France. The CMO could propose capable SMEs in Chiang Mai and Chiang Rai to carry out testing in Thailand for firms in other countries. It could also propose to CMOs abroad to carry out testing of new Thai products for their markets. In this case, Cosmetic Valley firms in France could carry out product testing of Thai products for the European market.

Other connections could also be made, for example between the Cosmetic Science Department in Chiang Rai University and the Cosmetic Valley cluster to learn from their activities and launch collaborative projects such as virtual seminars to build joint communities of practice.

Sources of further information: https://www.cosmetic-valley.com/

Arrangements for developing a cluster management organisation

It is recommended that the CMO become a member type organisation, as per the Minalogic global competitiveness cluster in Grenoble, France (see Box 4.2). Members could include SMEs, FDI, research organisations, skills development organisations as well as Government departments and agencies, including the OSMEP. As well as offering the benefits of networking, one of the incentives for participation offered by Minalogic is a label given to members. This is recognised by government departments and agencies and gives members the possibility to apply for publicly-subsidised collaborative R&D projects.

A CMO in Chiang Mai and Chiang Rai could be driven by a secretariat based in one of the regional knowledge organisations, such as the NSP. As the driver of the CMO, the NSP could work with the BOI in the attraction and aftercare of FDI, with the OSMEP brokering linkages between FDI and SMEs. It could also partner with other government agencies in brokering linkages with regional and national level universities and research organisations (including for example links with the BIOTEC national research laboratory).

The CMO could have a geographical boundary around the Chiang Mai and Chiang Rai provinces and target selected innovative start-ups and scale-ups in the advanced agriculture and biotechnology and food-for-the-future sectors as members. Only MNEs with regional direct investment presence could participate in the membership organisation.

The Federation of Thai Industries (FTI) plays an important role in promoting the agri-food cluster in Chiang Mai, with some 200 members in the food sector, following the model of the Food Valley ecosystem in the Netherlands. Thus the FTI is also a potential host for a CMO, and would in any case be a key player in the activities of any newly-created CMO.

Conclusions and policy recommendations

FDI activity is currently limited in advanced agriculture and biotechnology and food-for-the-future in Chiang Mai and Chiang Rai. This shows up in both the small scale of inward FDI and the limited linkages between FDI and SMEs and other cluster actors. Therefore FDI cannot be seen as a key anchor for knowledge generation and access to international markets for regional SMEs at the current juncture in the development of the cluster. However, the experience of biotechnology clusters internationally is that FDI can be expected to grow in parallel with the growth of the cluster. In other words, as the skills, research and SME capabilities in a biotechnology cluster grow, its attractiveness to FDI grows. Therefore FDI could become an important asset for the regional innovation cluster in the medium and long-term.

In order to stimulate such a positive development, policy needs to address the current lack of institutional arrangements in Chiang Mai and Chiang Rai for attracting and embedding FDI and for purposeful brokerage of FDI-SME linkages. Policies need to be introduced that can:

- build regional conditions that will attract FDI to Chiang Mai and Chiang Rai, including relevant research, training and capable SME suppliers;
- market the region to FDI, recognising the need to direct biotechnology-oriented FDI considering Thailand to Chiang Mai and Chiang Rai;
- create contacts with the FDI that has been attracted in terms of aftercare and connections to SMEs, universities, science parks, incubators and research organisations; and
- identify and support selected SMEs capable of working with FDI with upgrading their processes and management practices to the standards required by FDI and broker linkages between FDI and these SMEs.

This can be supported by the two policy approaches proposed above, namely:

1. Strengthening FDI policy for the advanced agriculture and biotechnology and food-for-the-future cluster in Chiang Mai and Chiang Rai through existing policy infrastructures.
2. Introducing FDI engagement activity in the activities of a CMO created for the Chiang Mai and Chiang Rai advanced agriculture and biotechnology and food-for-the-future cluster.

The key specific recommendations are put forward below.

Box 4.4. Recommendations on foreign direct investment

Strengthening FDI policy through existing policy infrastructures

- Develop a set of supporting conditions to attract FDI in advanced agriculture and biotechnology and food-for-the-future to Chiang Mai and Chiang Rai including by strengthening regional skills and research capabilities in this sector.
- Produce an on-line leaflet with the top-10 reasons why an inward FDI project in advanced agriculture and biotechnology and food-for-the-future will choose to locate in Chiang Mai and Chiang Rai and promote this with relevant FDI prospects.
- Steer advanced agriculture and biotechnology and food-for-the-future FDI projects exploring a location in Thailand to Chiang Mai and Chiang Rai, based on regional cluster mapping, and promoting the unique selling proposition of the regions for hosting FDI in these sectors.
- Reinforce BOI's linkages with other government departments and agencies and with regional organisations including the universities, science parks and cluster organisations players in promoting Chiang Mai and Chiang Rai to FDI.
- Increase the availability of incentives for FDI in advanced agriculture and biotechnology and food-for-the-future in Chiang Mai and Chiang Rai, for example by creating a Northern Corridor SEZ on the lines of the existing Eastern Corridor.
- Include promotion of FDI in regional innovation clusters as one of the core elements of the mission of the BOI working in collaboration with other agencies, including the OSMEP. This would involve:
    - Sharing data about stocks and flows of FDI in regional innovation clusters.
    - Marketing the strengths of regional innovation clusters to potential inward FDI.
    - Carrying out FDI aftercare at regional level.
    - Brokering connections between FDI and potential SME suppliers in regional innovation clusters.
    - Undertaking a regional pilot exercise in Chiang Mai and Chiang Rai involving (i) formation of an FDI-SME linkage strategy team, (ii) gathering and presenting data on the cluster, (iii) undertaking developmental actions including formalising networks and contacts with FDI, (iv) undertaking remedial actions to help FDI work through any regulatory barriers they face, (v) undertaking pilot actions to create some initial FDI-SME supply linkages with one or more inward investors.

FDI engagement through a new Cluster Management Organisation

- Create a CMO with a team of dedicated staff at the level of the advanced agriculture and biotechnology and food-for-the-future regional innovation cluster in Chiang Mai and Chiang Rai as a whole, with firms, universities, science parks and other organisations participating as CMO members.
- Include FDI attraction, aftercare and brokering linkages between FDI and SMEs and research organisations as part of the responsibilities of the CMO.
- Identify FDI operations hosted in the region with relevance to the cluster and develop FDI aftercare relationships with them. This includes establishing regular contacts between the public sector and FDI investments that would support FDI to overcome any operational problems locally, for example with regulations, and to promote reinvestment and contributions to regional cluster development.

- Create an easily accessible and usable, public and continuously updated web-based database of capable potential SME suppliers to FDI in advanced agriculture and biotechnology and food-for-the-future in Chiang Mai and Chiang Rai, including a range of company details such as locations, size and products and services.
- Co-ordinate an integrated package of consultancy, finance, training and innovation support to high potential SMEs with the capabilities to supply FDI in advanced agriculture and biotechnology and food-for-the-future in Chiang Mai and Chiang Rai to upgrade their capacities to supply FDI, together with support in winning supply contracts.
- Co-ordinate the offer of financial incentives to CMO members for participation in collaborative R&D projects as an incentive to FDI, SMEs, universities, science parks and others to get involved in applied research and its commercialisation and to build a culture of trust and collaboration amongst the players.
- Encourage the role of FDI in supporting corporate entrepreneurship and supporting incubators and other entrepreneurship support programmes in the cluster.
- Make links for cluster SMEs with FDI in related biotechnology clusters internationally

References

Assimakopoulos, D., M. Tsouri, D. Mavridis, and A. Moore, (2016), "Don't lose sight of the forest for the trees: Minalogic and Presto Engineering as a 'New Argonaut' in a French ICT ecosystem", 251-272 in Wang, H. and Y. Liu (eds.), *Entrepreneur and Talent Management from a Global Perspective: Global Returnees*, Edward Elgar, Cheltenham.

Assimakopoulos, D., H. Lawton Smith, N. Baines, M. Tsouri, and S. Romeo (forthcoming), "Oxford and Grenoble: knowledge organisations in local development revisited", *Regional Studies*, October 1 2021.

Berghall, E., (2017), "Knowledge spillovers, the technology frontier and high-tech FDI: evidence from Finland", *Finnish Economic Papers*, 28(1): 34-49, Finnish Economic Association, Autumn.

Blakely, E.J., and K.W. Willoughby (1990), "Transfer or generation? Biotechnology and local-industry development", *Journal of Technology Transfer*, 15(4): 31-38

De Propis, L., and N. Driffield (2006), "The importance of clusters for spillovers from foreign direct investment and technology sourcing", *Cambridge Journal of Economics*, 30(2): 277-291

Lefebvre, P. (2013), "Organising deliberate innovation in knowledge clusters: from accidental brokering to purposeful brokering processes", *International Journal of Technology Management*, 63 (3/4), 212 - 243.

Nowotny, H., P. Scott, and M. Gibbons (2003), "'Mode 2' Revisited: the new production of knowledge", Minerva, 41: 179-194

Potter, J. (2009), "The micro-nanotechnology cluster of Grenoble, France", in J. Potter and G. Miranda (eds) *Clusters, Innovation and Entrepreneurship*, OECD Publications, Paris https://dx.doi.org/10.1787/9789264044326-4-en

Saha, D. and K. Fikri, (2014), "*Cultivate Clusters as a Tool for an Effective FDI Strategy*", 7 August 2014 (accessed online on 6 February 2020) https://www.brookings.edu/blog/the-avenue/2014/08/07/cultivate-clusters-as-a-tool-for-an-effective-fdi-strategy /

Thompson, E. (2002), "Clustering of Foreign Direct Investment and Enhanced Technology Transfer:

Evidence from Hong Kong Garment Firms in China", *World Development*, 30(5): 873-889.

UNCTAD, *World Investment Report* 2019 (and various years)

World Economic Forum, *Global Competitiveness Reports* (2019 and various years)

Yehoue, E. B. (2005), "Clusters as a Driving Engine for FDI", IMF WP/2005/193, October, International Monetary Fund, Washington DC. See also http://www.clusterobservatory.in/articles/Article%20No.%2048.pdf

5 Clusters and new industry path development

This chapter examines new industry path development opportunities in advanced agriculture and biotechnology and food-for-the-future in Chiang Mai and Chiang Rai. These can occur through the integration of scientific biotechnology knowledge in the products of start-ups and scale-ups together with integration of engineering and marketing knowledge in these firms. A regional cluster management organisation could enable the exploitation of these opportunities by creating linkages between SMEs and universities and research organisations for the exchange of knowledge to promote new product development and sales.

Introduction

SMEs in Thailand show the following problematic characteristics (according to OECD, 2011):

- A "missing middle" – i.e. a shortage of medium-sized firms with the capability to grow. This limits the innovativeness and competitiveness of the SME sector and its potential to participate in national and global value chains and to co-operate with large firms and universities.
- An overly large share of entrepreneurs driven by necessity rather than by opportunity. These "necessity" entrepreneurs often have weak productivity and absorptive capacity for innovation, lack growth potential and suffer from low incomes and poor employment conditions.
- A large gap in the level of entrepreneurship and SME activity between the higher-income central region and the other regions of the country. Entrepreneurial activity in the regions is about one-half the rate of Bangkok. Similarly, around two-fifths of recorded SMEs are located in Bangkok region and its surrounds, where only one-tenth of the population lives. This weak SME and entrepreneurship activity is likely to hold back the catch up of other regions with Bangkok as well as the development trajectory of the country as a whole.
- A large brain drain from peripheral regions to Bangkok, which makes it difficult to retain educated youth with a bachelor degree in the Northern cities of Chiang Mai (even if this is the second largest city in Thailand) and Chiang Rai.

This chapter focuses on how cluster policy actions at regional level can help overcome these problems at the same time as developing higher value-added industry development trajectories in Thailand. It takes the case of the advanced agriculture and biotechnology and food-for-the-future regional innovation cluster in Chiang Mai and Chiang Rai. The analysis emphasises the importance of supporting start-ups and scale-ups in the cluster to develop and exploit advanced agricultural products, based in particular on biotechnology as a key enabling technology (KET), and proposes how to design appropriate cluster policies to support them.

Box 5.1 presents the relevance of the cluster concept for organising policy interventions to support the contribution of SMEs to new industry path development at regional level. It stresses the importance of seeing agglomerated regional clusters as being embedded within non-agglomerated national clusters, and the importance of start-ups and scale-ups to exploit the knowledge generated by universities and research organisations regionally and nationally. It shows how an expanded cluster policy in Chiang Mai and Chiang Rai is relevant to the objective of upgrading and diversifying its advanced agriculture and biotechnology and food-for-the-future industries.

Box 5.1. The relevance of cluster policies

Changing terminologies in regional innovation policies

A range of terms have been used in recent years to refer to policies that seek to build regional agglomeration economies to stimulate innovation and entrepreneurship. They include work on regional innovation systems, regional innovative milieux and clusters. While the terms come in and out of fashion, governments across the world are supporting various aspects of the development agglomeration economies. These policies have a strong emphasis on creating conditions for knowledge generation, exchange and exploitation in given sectors and regions. This report refers to these actions as cluster policies.

Cluster policies remain at the forefront of policy thinking about how to stimulate agglomeration economies in OECD countries. For example, most European Union countries have developed regional smart specialisation strategies identifying their areas of future industrial competitive advantage and how they will support them with innovation and entrepreneurship measures. These strategies are currently in the process of being updated for the new EU programming period 2021-27. These interventions can potentially support multiple clusters in a given region, if the region has a sufficiently diverse and specialised economy.

The best practice cluster interventions tend to see the regional clusters as being embedded in broader geographically-disaggregated clusters at national or international levels and to focus on promoting diversification of the clusters into higher value-added activities.

The relevance of regional agglomeration economies

Marshall is often referred to as the first scholar using the idea of industrial clustering. He argued that specialised industrial districts dominated by SMEs and embedded in the structures of society can be very competitive by generating and exploiting localisation economies, i.e. advantages from co-location of industries belonging to the same or supporting sectors (as opposed to urbanisation economies involving co-location of different sectors) (Asheim, 2000).

In his key 1998 article in Harvard Business Review, Porter focused on this kind of regional cluster, constituted by "geographic concentrations of interconnected companies and institutions in a particular field. Clusters encompass an array of linked industries and other entities important to competition. They include, for example, suppliers of specialised inputs such as components, machinery, and services, and providers of specialised infrastructure. Clusters also often extend downstream to channels and customers and laterally to manufacturers of complementary products and to companies in industries related by skills, technologies, or common inputs" (Porter 1998, 78).

The importance of non-agglomerated knowledge spillovers in national clusters

As a result of the growing complexity and diversity of contemporary knowledge creation and innovation processes, firms increasingly need to acquire new knowledge to supplement their internal, core knowledge. They can do this either by attracting human capital with different knowledge or by acquiring new knowledge by collaborating with external firms or universities and research institutes through R&D co-operation, outsourcing or offshoring of R&D. Thus a shift is taking place to a greater reliance on globally 'distributed knowledge networks' and 'open innovation' (Chesbrough, 2003). The absorptive capacity of SMEs is very important in the latter process as well as access to other players in national clusters.

In his 1990 book on 'Competitive Advantage of Nations', Porter referred mainly to non-agglomerated industrial clusters, arguing that "a nation's successful industries are usually linked through vertical (buyer/supplier) or horizontal (common customers, technology etc.) relationships" (Porter 1990, 149), even if some of the case studies (e.g. industrial districts in the 'Third Italy') referred to agglomerated regional clusters. This type of clustering remains important today.

The emphasis on knowledge exploitation

The general strength of the cluster concept is that it has a strong firm focus. Firms in clusters can be seen to constitute the knowledge exploitation sub-sector of a regional innovation system. The exploitation sub-sector connects to the knowledge exploration sub-sector, which consists largely of universities, research organisations, science parks and technology transfer organisations.

The dual emphasis of cluster policies

Recent applications of the cluster concept in policy in OECD countries focus on both strengthening regional agglomerated clusters and building linkages in national/international non-agglomerated clusters, where regional clusters are seen as being part of national clusters. This dual definition of clusters is becoming more important as a consequence of globalisation and digital technologies.

The importance of cluster diversification

In addition, the cluster concept and cluster policies are evolving to focus not on supporting existing in-situ industry specialisations, but on identifying opportunities to diversify existing specialisations into more innovative and higher value creating activities, in relation to the existing industries in the region as well as with respect to industries in other regions.

The key focus of modern cluster policies

These two key features of the modern concept of clusters and cluster policy fit well with the regional innovation situation in Thailand, namely the focus on :

- Supporting both regionally-agglomerated linkages (including knowledge exchanges) and national and internationally non-agglomerated linkages through clusters.

Thailand's cluster policy today supports both national and regional clusters. Thus the national advanced agriculture and biotech clusters, Food Innopolis and Thailand Food Valley, are constituted by regional clusters, which are supported by linkages to a national research centre of biotechnology.

- Supporting the diversification of regional and national industry specialisations into higher value-added and more innovative activities where a region can achieve future competitive advantage.

This requirement of industrial diversification fits very well with the cluster strategy of the national and regional cluster policy in Thailand of upgrading and diversifying agricultural production to become more advanced and innovative.

A key feature of clusters which cluster policies seek to promote according to this logic include (see also Porter, 2000):

- Innovation collaborations regionally and nationally and internationally, including among firms, universities and research institutes, particularly where they promote industrial diversification.
- The development of a specialised labour market providing cluster firms with skilled labour.

A well-functioning cluster management organisation (CMO) is a key component of an effective cluster policy. The CMO increases the absorptive capacity of SMEs by facilitating co-operation among firms in a cluster when approaching knowledge-generating institutions in the exploration sub-sector of the regional innovation system. In addition, being part of a national cluster increases the efficiency of cluster co-operation for SMEs as it provides easier access to important national R&D resources as well as regional resources.

Recent international policy experience with innovation clusters

During recent years, 'clustering' has increasingly been recognised as a pivotal tool for innovation policy. This includes policy interventions at the level of the European Union. Clusters have increasingly been taken into consideration in the definitions of the fundamental European Union innovation and regional development programmes, such as the European Structural and Investment Funds, H2020, COSME, etc., and are a key element in implementing smart specialisation (S3) policy. It also includes a wide range of recent cluster policy interventions in individual countries, such as Austria, Norway, and Sweden (see Boxes 5.2-5.4).

Relevance of the cluster concept for innovation policy in Thailand

The cluster concept is very useful for highlighting how policy can reinforce the role of firms in exploiting knowledge generated in Thailand's strategic sectors for future innovation-based growth, by creating regional and national knowledge linkages and building relevant regional skills and SME absorptive capacities. It can help to diversify cluster activities into higher value-added activities and to develop industrial competitiveness in areas outside the high-income core metropolitan region of the country.

In Chiang Mai and Chiang Rai, there is co-operation between regional universities, science parks and firms in advanced agriculture and biotechnology and food-for-the-future. Cluster policy is important to facilitate this co-operation by overcoming the problem of lack of absorptive capacity in SMEs with limited human and financial resources for innovation and lack of internal R&D capacities, and by helping build regional skills and knowledge networks.

New industry path development opportunities in Chiang Mai and Chiang Rai

Table 5.1 describes the main types of industry path development possible in regions and their mechanisms. Using this typology, Chiang Mai and Chiang Rai can realistically aim to achieve the following types of new industry path development:

- Path upgrading (through climbing Global Production Networks, Renewal, and/or niche development).
- Path importation.
- Unrelated diversification.

The region has clear opportunities for path upgrading and path importation, as discussed below. However, the most powerful of the path development opportunities in advanced agriculture and biotechnology and food-for-the-future in Chiang Mai and Chiang Rai is unrelated diversification, also discussed below. The main emphasis of policy for advanced agriculture and biotechnology and food-for-the-future should be on promoting unrelated diversification.

Table 5.1 Types of new regional industrial path development

Types	Mechanisms
Upgrading	
I – Climbing Global Production Networks	Major change of a regional industrial path related to enhancement of position within global production networks; moving up the value chain based on upgrading of skills and production capabilities
II – Renewal	Major change of an industrial path into a new direction based on new technologies or organisational innovations, or new business models
III – Niche development	Development of niches through the integration of symbolic knowledge
Diversification	
I – Related	Diversification into a new related industry for the region, building on competencies and knowledge of existing industries
II – Unrelated	Diversification into a new industry based on unrelated knowledge combinations
Emergence	
I – Importation	Setting up of an established industry that is new to the region (e.g. through non-local firms) and unrelated to exiting industries in the region.
II –New creation	Emergence and growth of entirely new industries based on radically new technologies and scientific discoveries or as an outcome of search processes for new business models, user-driven innovation and social innovation

Source: Based on Grillitsch, Asheim, and Trippl (2018) and Isaksen, Tödtling, and Trippl (2016)

Opportunities for path upgrading and path importation

The following opportunities can be pursued for path upgrading and path importation in the cluster.

Path upgrading by renewal or climbing global production networks

Path upgrading by moving firms up the value chain is achievable in advanced agriculture and biotechnology and food-for-the-future in Chiang Mai and Chiang Rai by introducing new technologies (e.g. Industry 4.0) and major organisational changes, including upgrading skills and production capabilities in SMEs. Being part of a dynamic cluster will boost this development.

Path upgrading by niche development

Path upgrading is also possible in the cluster through niche development in mature industries. An example of this taking place in advanced agriculture and biotechnology and food-for-the-future in Chiang Mai and Chiang Rai is the promotion of organic agriculture and food production. This has been driven by the use of symbolic, intangible knowledge in the marketing of the products. This could be for example in the form of story-telling about the history of the product, the environment in which it is being grown etc. (i.e. marketing innovation).

Path importation

Path importation to the Chiang Mai and Chiang Rai advanced agriculture and biotechnology and food-for-the-future cluster can be achieved through successfully attracting FDI and an inflow of skilled individuals with competences and production capabilities not available in the region. The successful national biotech strategy, and the competences at the regional universities and science parks, increase the attractiveness of Chiang Mai and Chiang Rai for foreign firms and individuals. The development of strong cluster policy actions will also increase the region's attractiveness.

However, these strategies are not as radical in terms of path development as strategies for unrelated diversification. They are more likely to lead to 'path extension', which is the outcome of incremental innovations in firms, which may result in stagnation and decline (path exhaustion) (Isaksen and Trippl 2016).

Opportunities for unrelated diversification in the cluster

The opportunities for unrelated diversification in the cluster offer the greatest steps towards diversifying the economy into more technologically-advanced specialisations that move up the ladder of higher knowledge complexity and value creation compared to the present level in the region. They should therefore be the main focus of the cluster policy efforts.

Unrelated diversification involves firms moving into new industries or areas of production by combining their existing knowledge bases with new, unrelated knowledge. The food industry in Chiang Mai and Chiang Rai can be characterised as a traditional industry based on synthetic, engineering knowledge. However, start-ups and scale-ups can combine this knowledge with new analytical, science-based knowledge in KETs (particularly biotechnology, but also nanotechnology and digitalisation) to diversify into advanced agricultural products, functional food and beverages, food-for-the-future, medical food and cosmetics. Internationally, the introduction of science-based, analytical knowledge from biotechnology has led to the generation of high value-added functional foods with particular health benefits (Zukauskaite and Moodysson, 2016), and there are firms in Chiang Mai and Chiang Rai that are already doing this, supported by the national and regional food clusters.

The outlook for future unrelated diversification in Chiang Mai and Chiang Rai is very promising. On the demand side, there is an almost unlimited international market for safe and healthy food, functional food and beverages, non-chemical plant and herb-based medicine and cosmetic products. On the supply side, Northern Thailand seems to have the natural resources and scientific knowledge to successfully develop products to meet this demand. Overall, the food and beverage industry in Thailand contributes 23% of GDP and Chiang Mai and Chiang Rai have key agricultural production and processing specialisations in vegetables, fruits and herbal products. Thailand, both nationally and in the Chiang Mai and Chiang Rai regions, also has the knowledge exploration capabilities in KETs – in particular biotechnology, together with nanotechnology and digitalisation – that are critical to generate new and advanced agricultural products in start-ups and scale-ups, particularly in functional foods.[1]

Longan is a good example of how biotechnology can be integrated in agricultural products to increase their value. Longan contains a number of active, healthy ingredients, and research aimed at extracting compounds from longan seeds is ongoing at several universities, which are seeking to develop other important by-products to be used for medical purposes. For example, in the Northern Food Valley, biotechnology is being used to produce an anti-aging agent. In another case, a functional food is being produced in the form of a beverage to help sleeping, based on research conducted by Chiang Rai University in co-operation with Natural Beverage Corporation, Ltd.

There are also examples of using research in biotechnology to add value to other agricultural products in Chiang Mai and Chiang Rai:

- A start-up called Sleep Well manufactures beverages that aid sleep using vanilla and honey.
- Tofusun produces bed-time milk from soybeans fortified with melatonin to aid sleep.
- A start-up called Morinaga produces a candy with lactic acid bacteria to prevent the common cold.
- A tech start-up called Juiceinno8, and funded by TukTuk500 Venture Capital, produces fruit juice without natural sugar to help prevent diabetes.
- The Tea Gallery Group, a group of SMEs in Chiang Mai, produces fermented tea, called "Kombucha", with documented health benefits including reduced cholesterol, blood pressure, inflammation, migraines and fatigue.

Unrelated diversification in advanced agriculture and biotechnology and food-for-the-future in Chiang Mai and Chiang Rai can build on the actions of the Thailand Industrial Development Strategy 4.0. This targets a broad set of "s-curve", "locomotive" industries and aims to help them grow by supporting the introduction of advanced technology and innovation, in particular in SMEs. In the case of advanced agriculture and biotechnology and food-for-the-future, the policy targets applications of research in functional food, medical food, food supplements and food innovation, as these are among the most dominant industries in Northern Thailand, as well as in biofuels and bio-chemicals and medical, health and cosmetics products made from herbs and plants. These sectors are also supported by Thailand's National Biotechnology Policy Framework 2012-2021, which targets agriculture and food, medicine and public health, bio energy, and bio industries.

The Thailand Industrial Development Strategy 4.0 and the National Biotechnology Policy Framework are successfully building Thailand's research capacity in biotechnology. There are a number of key components to this:

- The National Centre for Genetic Engineering and Biotechnology (BIOTEC), established in 1983, has multiple laboratories for conducting research and providing technical services in agricultural, biomedical and environmental sciences. For example, the BIOTEC Food Biotechnology Laboratory helps improve and upgrade the processing and quality of traditional Thai fermented food.
- The National Science and Technology Development Agency (NSTDA) acts as a bridge between research in BIOTEC and industry. It does this by providing resources to industry to develop a critical mass of industry researchers to apply biotechnological research in product and process innovations. NSTDA has focused on five target sectors, including agriculture and food, energy and environment and health and medicine.
- The regional universities in Chiang Mai and Chiang Rai undertake applied research directed to developing applications for local industry.
- The regional science parks (especially NSP) play a key role in applied R&D, connecting universities with industry. At NSP, for example, specialists and researchers from industry, universities and NSTDA collaborate to develop biotechnology applications to be exploited by regional industry. NSP is part of a system of Thailand Science Parks (TSPs), which further serve as a one-stop service centre to assist foreign and domestic firms engaged in scientific and technological research.

It may be rather surprising that Thailand, as a middle-income country, has developed cutting-edge biotechnology research in many areas with a strong focus on application. However, Thailand's effort to build a strong biotechnology research capacity must be seen in the context of the country's position as a global leader in agriculture and as one of the top exporters of food in the world. This led to a strategic decision to transform agriculture into a knowledge-based industry using biotechnology as a KET with applications in agriculture and the aquatic field, but also beyond in the medical and industrial (e.g. bioeconomy) sectors.

Similar use of biotechnology as a KET has been seen in several high-income countries in the last ten years. Several European countries have developed industrial policies at national level to support biotechnology, and several European Union regions have included advanced agriculture and food-for-the-future as part of their regional smart specialisation (S3) strategies.

Thus Thailand has embarked on industrial and innovation policies that are broadly state-of-the-art internationally. These policies are not only a set of "paper plans", but have been implemented and are starting to produce promising results. Thailand has demonstrated exemplary policy design by building up an advanced basic research capacity in biotechnology at BIOTEC in Bangkok directed towards applications in sectors that are of significant importance for the Thai economy and linking it to applied research at regional universities and science parks located in proximity to the regional firms and specialisations that should integrate the new technologies to advance their products and processes, e.g. agriculture and food in Chiang Mai and Chiang Rai.

However, the missing link in the current arrangements to develop the advanced agriculture and biotechnology and food-for-the-future strategic sectors in Thailand is a more effective cluster policy that can increase the absorptive capacity of start-ups and scale-ups and put them in a position to exploit the produc-relevant research results being generated nationally and regionally. A policy is needed that:

- effectively introduces scientific and marketing knowledge to start-ups and scale-ups in order to secure the exploitation of research; and
- operates in regions outside of the capital region in order to spread the economic growth generated.

These are the major missing pieces in the policy puzzle that will help unlock the potential of SMEs for the development of the s-curve, strategic driving sectors at regional level in Thailand. The potential design of this policy is discussed in the section below.

Developing a regional cluster policy for Chiang Mai and Chiang Rai

There are two main components of the proposed cluster development policy for advanced agriculture and biotechnology and food-for-the-future in Chiang Mai and Chiang Rai regions:

- creation of an overarching cluster management organisation (CMO); and
- introduction of direct cluster development actions for the regional innovation cluster (in addition to the existing tax incentives for innovation).

Adequate and long-term funding is required for these actions. For example, funding is made available to supported clusters for 10 years in Norway and Sweden, where the support comes partly from government and partly from matching funding from the other triple helix stakeholders (research and business actors) participating in the cluster. Adopting the principle of matching funding brings a strong commitment by the stakeholders to seriously engage in systematic and long-term co-operation to promote innovativeness and increased (global) competitiveness.

Creation of a cluster management organisation

The creation of an overarching cluster management organisation (CMO) aims to create a structure to:

- create new networks and collaborations between start-ups and scale-ups and universities, science parks and research laboratories to help start-ups and scale-ups acquire new and more advanced technology;
- increase the knowledge absorption capacities of start-ups and scale-ups by offering advice and coaching and supplier development programmes; and

- help create an overall shared vision and development plan for the cluster by bringing together cluster stakeholders to discuss challenges and plans.

A CMO can be seen as a formal organisation, including a set of cluster management agents who undertake actions to create networks and co-operations between participants in the cluster. The cluster management agents can play the role of account managers working with specific firms and research organisations to identify their development needs and collaboration opportunities.

In addition, some of the specific roles that the CMO can play are discussed in chapters 2-4 with respect to developing a vision for regional entrepreneurship development in the cluster and co-ordinating policy actions in this area, targeting higher-quality business development services (BDS) on start-ups and scale-ups with innovation and export potential in the cluster, and attracting FDI to the cluster and supporting the development of FDI-SME linkages in the cluster as the scale of the FDI grows.

The CMO should also undertake vision building and strategy development work for the cluster. This should be undertaken through a bottom-up Entrepreneurial Discovery Process (as referred to in the European Union Smart Specialisation Policy) involving ideas generation and consensus building by regional entrepreneurs in business and institutional entrepreneurs at universities, research organisations and science parks, as well as regional and local government authorities to identify projects to support the development of the cluster. The CMO can help combine this local vision with top-down national government policies.

Direct expenditure and long term financial support is required to build a strong CMO for advanced agriculture and biotechnology and food-for-the-future in Chiang Mai and Chiang Rai. Much of the current cluster networking work undertaken by the existing small-scale cluster initiatives in Chiang Mai and Chiang Rai appears to be undertaken as unpaid work outside of normal working hours. This makes it difficult to put enough time into developing the clusters to fulfil their potential and leads to important tasks not being carried out or carried out too slowly. It also reduces the commitment of firms participating in the cluster initiatives to engage wholeheartedly in developing the clusters.

Direct cluster capacity-building actions

In addition to the creation of a CMO and cluster management agents, direct funding is needed for cluster firms to participate in a range of projects that will increase their innovation and exporting activities. One of the main areas for this funding is for applied research projects undertaken by research organisations, which could be undertaken on behalf of selected groups of start-ups and scale-ups.

Thailand's existing cluster policy initiatives offer support that is largely indirect and available in a non-targeted manner. The main existing initiative is Thailand's Cluster-based Special Economic Development Zones Policy, which came into effect in 2015 and is led by the Ministry of Industry. This offers tax and non-tax incentives to companies for R&D and innovation investments in co-operation with academic institutions or other research organisations in specific sectors and locations in the country. There are two types of cluster: Super Clusters and Other targeted clusters.

- Super Clusters include 'first s-curve' industries, e.g. automotive and parts and smart electronics, which develop by using advanced technology, and 'new s-curve' industries, which involve future industries (e.g. robotics and medical hub). Food Innopolis is one of the first-wave Super Clusters, and the only representative of agriculture and biotechnology.[2] It is a national initiative built up of regional clusters with different industrial specialisations. It is expanding to regional science parks, among them the Northern Science Park in Chiang Mai, which will focus on rice, fruits, vegetables and organic products, and is financing co-operations with a range of regional universities in these areas.
- Other targeted clusters include the Thailand Food Valley agro-processing cluster, which was established in 2014 to support SMEs in the advanced agriculture and food sectors in

collaboration with the Ministry of Agriculture and Cooperatives, Department of Industrial Work, Ministry of Science and Technology, Thai Chamber of Commerce and the Federation of Thai Industries. The cluster focuses on sustainability, improving the value chain, food quality, increasing exports, and bringing technology and innovation to the sector (www.behance.net). Launched in 2016, Chiang Mai is the first pilot location for the Thailand Food Valley programme, defined as Northern Food Valley 1, including a focus on coffee ("the city of coffee") as an important sub-sector, while Chiang Rai will belong to Northern Food Valley 2, with tea ("the city of tea") as a sub-sector (www.northernfoodvalley2.com).

The downside of the strong reliance of these programmes on R&D tax incentives is that they are provided to all firms in sectors and regions designated as clusters. The incentives may therefore go both to firms in need of this support, and firms that would have undertaken the subsidised R&D and innovation activities without the support. In addition, start-ups and scale-ups very often only generate a taxable surplus after some years of operation, which means that in the first years, when they are in most need of support, they do not have any advantage from tax exemption.[3] These issues reduce the effectiveness of tax incentives as a cluster development measure.

In addition, support needs to be introduced that is focused more on networking and capacity-building for selected firms with strong growth potential. These activities, for example, could include training programmes to increase the absorptive capacity of cluster firms, R&D projects between cluster firms and universities and science parks, and creating meeting places locally, regionally and nationally for learning and knowledge exchange among firms. They could also include business advisory services and supplier development programmes. In addition, cluster firms could identify needs-driven R&D projects that could be funded for groups of start-ups and scale-ups.

In designing these activities much can be learned from successful cluster development policies in Norway and Sweden presented in Box 5.2-Box 5.3 below.

Box 5.2. Norwegian Innovation Cluster Programme, Norway

Description of the approach

The Norwegian Innovation Cluster programme aims to increase the attractiveness and dynamics of clusters in Norway, improve the innovativeness and competitiveness of individual companies within clusters, and trigger and enhance collaborative development activities in clusters. It is organised by Innovation Norway (the public innovation agency), in collaboration with Siva (the public industrial development corporation of Norway) and the Norwegian Research Council.

The programme was launched in June 2014, building on a national cluster policy that has evolved since the early 2000s. It adds new levels, modules and elements to the pre-existing Arena and the Norwegian Centres of Expertise (NCE) programmes in order to further develop existing and potential new cluster initiatives.

Important distinctions are made in the programme between a cluster, a cluster organisation and a cluster development project, with support being targeted at cluster development projects and cluster organisations in order to improve the performance of the clusters:

- *A cluster* is seen as a geographical concentration of enterprises and related knowledge communities linked by complementarity or a similarity of interests and needs. The enterprises in the cluster can gain easier access to important production factors and ideas for and impulses to innovation through interaction and co-operation. A cluster emerges over time, on the basis of location advantages and natural dynamics.
- *A cluster organisation* is a formal institution that is established to facilitate increased interaction and co-operation between participants in the cluster. A cluster organisation is based on an organised partnership between the participants in the cluster, often with public development agencies as important contributors.
- *A cluster development project* is a targeted effort over a limited period to strengthen and accelerate the development of the cluster. This is generally achieved by means of a wide range of strategic activities aimed at strengthening the cluster's and cluster participants' competitive position.

Clusters compete to be part of the programme through annual open calls for funded cluster development projects. There are strict selection criteria for a cluster to be able to participate in the programme. The cluster resources, potential for growth and position in the industry is important. However, just as important is the participation and leadership of enterprises in the cluster project, i.e. the proposed initiative must be led by enterprises and meet their common interests and have their common ownership. In evaluating the applications for project funding, the emphasis is set on how far the enterprises of the cluster have set their strategic goals for collaboration and growth and how they have made their common plans for implementation of the cluster development project.

The programme distinguishes between clusters on three levels – providing different strands of programme support:

Arena (*Immature clusters*): Clusters that are in an early phase of organised cluster collaboration. They can vary significantly in their pre-conditions and potential. They can be small or large, and the participants can be in a regional, national or international competitive position.

Norwegian Centres of Expertise (*Mature clusters with a national position*): Clusters that have already established systematic and dynamic collaborations among their participants with high interaction and a broad strategic action area. The enterprises in these clusters have considerable potential for growth in national and international markets.

Global Centres of Expertise ***(Mature clusters with a global position)***: As with the Norwegian Centres of Expertise, these clusters have already established systematic and dynamic collaborations among their participants with high interaction and a broad strategic action area and the cluster enterprises have considerable potential for growth in national and international markets. However, in addition, these clusters form part of a strong innovation system, including privately-funded R&D by the participants and not only publicly-funded R&D.

The clusters are supported with partial funding for a cluster management organisation, as well as advisory services, cluster development support, networking activities and profiling services. The Arena support is given over 3-5 years, whereas the Norwegian Centres of Expertise and Global Centres of Expertise give support over a 10 year period. There are annual evaluations of the activities of each cluster determining whether they are on the right track according to the strategies they put forward for funding and whether they deliver at sufficiently high quality to continue as part of the programme.

Factors for success

The Norwegian Innovation Clusters has received positive evaluations by national and international experts. The most important factors behind this success are: 1) the three levels of clusters, which make cluster organisation open to firms of all sizes and phases of development, as well as the possible progression between the levels; 2) the long term and quite generous funding of the cluster management organisations and other forms of strategic cluster assistance through the cluster development projects; 3) the strict criteria for selection of clusters to become members of the programme, where the emphasis is on the common ownership of stakeholders in the cluster project as well as the yearly evaluations of the progress of the cluster development strategies.

Obstacles encountered and responses

The main obstacles that have been encountered to the success of the programme lie either in a lack of cluster resources (the critical mass of participating firms was not large enough; firms of critical importance withdraw from the cluster project) or in a leadership at firm and cluster levels that was not strong and/or motivated enough to develop the cluster. Responses to these problems have been either to terminate the cluster project before its originally envisaged end-date or to use more strategic support (other than economic funding) to resolve the obstacles encountered.

Relevance for Chiang Mai and Chiang Rai regions

The Chiang Mai and Chiang Rai advanced agriculture and biotechnology and food-for-the-future cluster can be seen as corresponding to the first level of support provided by the Norwegian Innovation Clusters Programme – i.e. Arena (for immature clusters). Arena has been important in creating cluster management organisations and strategic cluster development projects in this type of cluster and has built positive momentum. It illustrates a type of approach that emphasises long-term and generous direct funding for cluster management organisations, advisory services for SMEs, and networking activities as well as R&D funding. This type of support could be added to the existing cluster policy in Thailand, which currently focuses on tax credits for investment. It also highlights the importance of a thorough selection process for supported clusters, the criteria applied for selection of clusters for support, and annual evaluations of the progress made in delivering the cluster strategies, which leads to withdrawal of support or remedial action in the case of missed objectives.

Sources of further information: https://www.innovationclusters.no/english

Box 5.3. Vinnväxt programme, Sweden

Description of the approach

Vinnväxt (Win Growth) is operated by Vinnova, Sweden's public innovation agency. Its mission is to support sustainable innovation-led regional growth through stimulating the emergence of internationally-competitive regional research and innovation environments targeting specific high value-creation growth industries.

The programme has issued five calls for proposals for institutional development and needs-driven R&D projects since its launch in 2001, the latest finalised in 2016. The funding is selective and awarded to regions through a competitive process. To be selected, the region must propose a strategic idea to develop clusters by forming collaborations with other sectors or technologies creating synergy effects and by exploiting key enabling technologies (KETs).

Some 230 regional development initiatives, each promoted by a set of regional stakeholders, have applied for funding under Vinnväxt's five calls. Of these, 18 "functional regions" have been selected for support. The winners share a number of common features including: a shared strategic concept among the regional cluster actors; a strong research and innovation milieu; strong regional leadership for the cluster development activity; and the active participation of the public (regional government), private (business and industry) and research (university and research organisations) sectors, namely all elements of the "Triple Helix". Perhaps the most important factor, however, is that all appear to have excellent growth potential.

Vinnväxt adopts a long-term outlook, providing winning regional initiatives with funding of up to EUR 1 million per year for 10 years. This funding can be extended in some cases up to as far as 16 years to help the regional initiative to bridge the transition from long-term public funding to other funding sources. The winning regions must contribute at least the same amount. The projects aim to support the development of infrastructure for innovation, rather than direct support to businesses. Furthermore, winners are offered 'process support' in the form of seminars, coaching, networking and experience sharing. The selected regional initiatives are evaluated every three years by international experts to ensure compliance with the terms of the programme.

From 2013, the programme has introduced a stronger focus on initiatives that support sustainable development, green growth and societal benefits.

Factors for success

Key factors for success have been:

- The long-term and generous public funding.
- The use of the collaboration among the Triple Helix actors (government, research and business) to develop shared policy proposals.
- The strong financial and other commitments of the Triple Helix constellation in the regions as part of the funding arrangements.
- The combination of support for knowledge exploration (research) and knowledge exploitation (innovation) and a strong focus on innovation and international competitiveness.
- The design of the programme as both a top-down and bottom-up initiative.

The programme has led to better enterprise development results in supported regional clusters; strengthened collaboration between universities, research institutes and industry in the clusters; and expanded R&D capacity in industry leading to product development. Vinnväxt has made the Triple Helix a well-known concept throughout Sweden, and has strengthened regional innovation systems and their support structures. In turn the Vinnväxt initiatives have taken significant steps in becoming internationally competitive and sustainable regional innovation environments.

Obstacles encountered and responses

The most common problems that have arisen for the programme in developing stronger and internationally-competitive regional research and innovation milieus have been when industry specialisations do not connect well to the existing research capacity of the region or when there is a lack of absorptive capacity in the regional industry, which implies that it cannot make use of and exploit the research results of the research organisations for innovation. Through evaluations of the regional initiatives every 3 years, such imbalances in the regional innovation system can be discovered and efforts put in place to try to correct them.

Relevance for Chiang Mai and Chiang Rai regions

This programme illustrates a long-term approach to supporting the development of regional innovation clusters. It illustrates how to engage regional actors in common vision building on the actions needed to support the development of the cluster by offering funding to bids put together by coalitions of Triple Helix actors. It also illustrates an approach to support the exploitation of KETs in SMEs by involving them in close co-operations between universities, research organisations and industry.

Sources for further information: https://www.vinnova.se

Further inspiration for developing a regional CMO and direct strategic support measures for cluster development in advanced agriculture and biotechnology and food-for-the-future in Chiang Mai and Chiang Rai can be drawn from the example of a cluster specifically focused on food innovation in the region of Scania in southern Sweden (Box 5.4).

Box 5.4. The Food Innovation at Interfaces Project, Scania, Southern Sweden

Description of the approach

The Food Innovation at Interfaces project is one of the regional initiatives funded by the national Vinnväxt programme supporting food innovation in a regional cluster in Scania, Sweden. It supported a large number of small-scale incremental innovations among food industry SMEs in the region in collaboration with the region's university, Lund University. Over time, this reoriented the regional industry towards higher value-added markets and increased exports.

The project was established by a partnership of firms, research organisations and local government organisations that came together to form the Scania Food Innovation Network (Skånes Livsmedelsakademi or SLA). The Network was originally created in 1994 with a membership encompassing university faculties, the regional government of Scania, dairy firms, and leading food production actors. Lund University is a key actor in the Network. Its representatives held several posts in the Board of Directors and it was a leading partner in several of the research projects.

The Network put together a successful application for support from the national Vinnväxt programme in 2001. This led to an award of government funding of EUR 2 million per annum for 10 years. To win this funding, the Network had to demonstrate a broad, supportive coalition of public and private sector actors with a track record of effective collaboration in innovation. Although the programme has now ended, the networks and linkages that it generated continue, involving Lund University, the regional science park and regional industry. The Scania Food Innovation Network continues to operate, and Vinnova still provides funding for specific projects, such as research on food for elderly health care.

The key issue that the project responded to was that although it had a combination of an existing food cluster and world-leading R&D in food, the SMEs in the regional food industry had very low levels of R&D and few connections with the region's research organisations. They had identifiable needs for knowledge inputs of different kinds that the regional university and other research organisations could supply to support them in product and process development. However, the typical inputs required from the University for each individual firm were very small and scattered across different university departments. These inputs were much smaller on average than the types of research contracts that the University typically dealt with and the university did not have experience of combining these needs into viable projects or collaborating with SMEs on individual small projects.

One of the issues for the University was that the knowledge inputs required for innovation stretched across a range of different academic disciplines. Particular firms could have simultaneous demands for science-based analytical knowledge (bio-sciences), engineering-based synthetic knowledge (mechanical engineering, automation) and symbolic knowledge (marketing, advertisement). Linkages therefore had to be made across various research departments of the University and needs aggregated into larger projects.

With the substantial government funding for this project, Lund University was able to prioritise supporting SMEs and becoming a linking node between appropriate sources of knowledge and expertise within the University and other regional partners.

Factors for success

A key success factor for this project was a decade of prior interactive network building in Scania around food innovation embodied in the Scania Food Innovation Network. This had generated a latent innovation network in which the University (as key knowledge supplier to SMEs) already played an important role.

The process of developing the funding application to the Vinnväxt programme was also coordinated and written by the Scania Food Innovation Network. The presence of the prior connections was one of the reasons for its selection for support by the national government.

The Vinnväxt programme itself provided the necessary funding to allow the University to engage with SMEs.

Obstacles encountered and responses

One of the obstacles to the development of the regional cluster was a lack of critical mass of collaborations in particular fields aggregating the needs of individual SMEs. This made it difficult for Lund University to respond to SME individual demands. One of the responses was to focus more strongly on one specific area of food and health – namely functional food – compared with the early focuses of the network on four areas; functional food; international consumer marketing; large-scale food and eating (for hospitals, schools, et.); and food innovation in theory and practice.

In order to reinforce the research and support to SMEs in functional food (i.e. to focus on creating foods with specific health giving properties) one of the key outputs of the funding was to create the Functional Food Science Centre at Lund University. This was a new wave university research centre involving 70 senior researchers from 40 departments and five faculties at Lund University. Funding from the programme helped establish a PhD curriculum within the Centre, delivered in close collaboration with the food industry and representatives of the commercial and industrial development and the health and medical care system in Scania.

In addition, there was no easy recipe to provide technology transfer to many small businesses directly without the requirement for individual researchers or research departments to create their own connections with SMEs and whilst ensuring that the university retained a strategic focus on core scientific activities.

In response, the university pursued a two-pronged approach:

- Intermediary organisations were enrolled in the network to relieve the necessity for Lund University to work directly with many small firms simultaneously. In addition, a new intermediary organisation was created called IDEON Agro Food, based at IDEON, a science park at the university. This applied the IDEON business support model, originally developed for exploiting ICT and biotech companies (using mainly analytical knowledge in high-technology fields) in the functional food area. IDEON Agro Food encouraged the formation of larger networks and better relationships between food companies and knowledge producers, using predominantly synthetic knowledge in low-technology fields.
- Lund University's success in winning strategic research projects focused academic leaders on thinking how to best engage with regional communities and businesses, to deliver the core university missions by providing access to core research funding, increasing their world-class status and visibility. Many of the activities of the Food Innovation at Interfaces programme had a dual basis, firstly in university research but also in wider university-centred – but nevertheless boundary-spanning – activities, which emerged as Lund University became regionally engaged.

Relevance for Chiang Mai and Chiang Rai regions

This initiative demonstrates a method to transform food production in a region from a mass-producing sector of low quality and low cost products to high quality products with a large value creation potential. It achieved this by creating networks of SMEs connected to a regional university with relevant knowledge, with the support of the science park as an intermediary.

The initiative had a particular emphasis on creating linkages between the different types of knowledge that SMEs need to develop functional foods, combining science, engineering and marketing inputs from the University. The emphasis on combining different types of knowledge is shared with the Clusterland Upper Austria case (Box 5.5). However, whereas Clusterland Upper Austria focuses on cross-fertilisation between clusters, in Scania the aim was to combine these different types of knowledge for SMEs within the same cluster. This is closer to the requirements of advanced agriculture and biotechnology and food-for-the-future in Chiang Mai and Chiang Rai, where the university and science park can bring packages of knowledge to networks of regional SMEs to support their innovation.

The case also demonstrates how to develop a network of stakeholders including SMEs, science parks and the university over the long term and the benefits this can have. The aim in Scania was to develop the Scania Food Innovation Network to become the best network globally for co-operation between the different knowledge areas and competences that will develop the food sector in the future. The work resulted in network co-operation and relations regionally, nationally and internationally between university, industry and research institutes.

The Network has had a strong focus on food and hospitality. During the years more than 120 firms have become members of the network, including large firms such as Tetra Pak and Findus. The initiative has resulted in more than 35 different products and services. Among the new or improved products developed are sport beverages, infection-reducing food (functional food), and various forms of nutrition additives. These represent to a large extent the same range of advanced agricultural products that are being promoted in Chiang Mai and Chiang Rai.

Source: Benneworth, P., L. Coenen, J. Moodysson, and B. T. Asheim, (2009), "Exploring the Multiple Roles of Lund University in Strengthening the Scania Regional Innovation System: Towards Institutional Learning?" *European Planning Studies*, 17(11), 1645-1664.

A national platform for clusters

It would also be useful in Thailand to create a platform for different regional clusters to exchange information and ideas and to network together. This platform can provide operational support for different clusters, as well as capacity-building support for professionals working in CMOs. It can also provide a platform to strengthen diversification projects involving firms and research institutions in different clusters. Box 5.5 sets out a model from Austria.

Box 5.5. The national Austrian Cluster Platform and the Upper Austria Clusterland Platform, Austria

Description of the approach

Austria was an early mover in policy to support regional cluster management organisations. The Automotive Cluster Styria was founded in the Syria region in 1995, the Automotive Cluster in Upper Austria was founded in 1998 and from 2000 onwards other regions followed. There are now more than 60 regional cluster management organisations in Austria with more than 7 100 cluster members (73% of them SMEs), accounting for some 815 000 employees. The cluster networks are linked up with research and educational institutions and co-operate with other clusters.

Cluster Platforms have been created at national and regional level to support information exchange, collaboration, cross-fertilisation and professional capacity building among the different regional cluster organisations. This case study covers the national platform for all the regional cluster management organisations nationally, and an example of a regional platform in the Upper Austria region, to help co-ordinate the different clusters within the region.

The national cluster platform

In 2008, the Federal Ministry of Science, Research and Economy launched the Austrian Cluster Platform as a structured strategic and working environment for cluster management organisations and networks in Austria. The goals are to increase co-operation between national and regional levels on support policies for clusters, especially for R&D and skills, to reinforce co-operation between clusters and research institutions, and to support information exchange and co-operation among the regional clusters and with foreign clusters.

The Platform plays an important role in supporting early and intensive information exchange across the country's cluster networks on best practices for improving cluster management. The Austrian Cluster Platform is responsible for the organisation of the annual Austrian Cluster Conference and maintains five working groups – on clusters in the national innovation system; cluster good practices related to research, innovation and skills; cluster-relevant developments in technology and innovation at European level, including regional policy; internationalisation of clusters; and future production technologies Industry 4.0 and Knowledge Intensive Services. The Platform provides regular information to the cluster network members. It also aims to participate in the development of European Union strategy and programme development to make the EU-wide initiatives relevant to the support of the regional clusters.

The regional cluster platform

A regional-level cluster platform called "Clusterland" has also been created in Upper Austria region to co-ordinate the different cluster programmes in the region. The Clusterland platform is funded and supported by the Upper Austria Business Agency, and has a Director and staff to support networking, information exchange and capacity building across the clusters. It co-ordinates nine clusters, each of which is represented on the governing board of the platform. The clusters are the Automotive Cluster; Plastics Cluster; Furniture and Timber Construction Cluster; Health Technology Cluster; Information Technology Cluster; Clean Tech Cluster; Food Cluster; Mechatronics Cluster; and Medical Technology Cluster.

This organisational set-up coordinates the various clusters in the region to facilitate cross-cluster co-operation and innovation through co-operation in the cross-roads of the clusters. This supports breaking out of the value chains of the individual clusters by looking out of the (cluster) box. This cross-fertilisation between different clusters facilitates and strengthens the innovative capacity and competitive advantage of regional innovation system and promotes growth in value added through cluster diversification.

Factors for success

These cluster platforms are very well organised and create strong horizontal links between clusters and vertical links between the national and regional innovation systems. The strong focus on cluster policy has been very important in strengthening the innovativeness, competitiveness and internationalisation of SMEs.

Obstacles encountered and responses

The problem of the absorptive capacity of SMEs is an issue in all advanced cluster programmes with a strong focus on SMEs, especially with respect to the aim of the cluster management organisations to improve connections between SMEs and R&D organisations. This problem has been addressed by the programmes in two ways. First, the national working groups enable learning and information exchange among the clusters on best practices for improving cluster management. Second, Austria has strong arrangements for supporting SME skills development through vocational training (competence building by training apprentices through the dual education/apprenticeship programmes) and placements of graduates from the universities and especially the applied universities in SMEs.

Relevance for Chiang Mai and Chiang Rai regions

The Austria cluster policies demonstrate an effective approach to co-ordinating activities across clusters and to sharing operational and capacity building support. They highlight how cluster platforms at the national and regional level can support both learning by cluster management organisations on best practice cluster support activities and cross-fertilisation between clusters for unrelated diversification and the integration of KETs. This type of platform can play an important role in linking together activities for the regional advanced agriculture and biotechnology and food-for-the-future cluster in Chiang Mai and Chiang Rai with the activities of other major strategic clusters in Thailand.

Sources for further information: www.biz-up.at

Conclusions and policy recommendations

There is strong potential to develop advanced agriculture and biotechnology and food-for-the-future in Chiang Mai and Chiang Rai using biotech as a KET. This is based on a successful national strategy to develop research in relevant areas with potential for commercialisation, including through BIOTEC and national and regional universities and research organisations. However, there is a missing link in terms of the exploitation of the research by SMEs in their products in international markets. One of the major responses to this should be the creation of a cluster management organisation and cluster development agents to create networks between SMEs and universities, research organisations and science parks and to provide support to entrepreneurs and firms with start-up and scale-up potential to integrate new technologies and improve their marketing and business organisation.

The existing cluster policy is not sufficient for this task. The policy focuses particularly on tax incentives for R&D and innovation projects with individual firms. This approach should be expanded to include the long-term funding of an overarching cluster management organisation for advanced agriculture and biotechnology and food-for-the-future in Chiang Mai and Chiang Rai. This organisation would support the creation of a vision for cluster development in consultation with cluster stakeholders, increase the visibility and marketing of the cluster, and undertake networking and brokering of connections between groups of SMEs and the universities, science parks and research organisations for technology transfer. It should also fund direct cluster support measures including direct financing of training programmes and collaborative R&D projects.

There are many international examples of cluster policies adopting this approach, some of them illustrated in the chapter, including within European Union regional smart specialisation strategies. Overall, a change in Thailand's cluster policy is required to support the absorption of knowledge generated through public research by start-up and scale-up SMEs. The key policy recommendations are presented below:

Box 5.6. Recommendations on clusters and new industry path development

- Continue the advanced national research on biotechnology as a key enabling technology (KET) and strengthen the focus of this research on potential areas of application of the technology in advanced agriculture products and food-for-the-future.
- Strengthen applied research in universities and development work in science parks in Chiang Mai and Chiang Rai in areas of applications of biotechnology in advanced agriculture products and food-for-the-future.
- Create a cluster management organisation (CMO) with cluster management agents for the cluster. The CMO should be a public-private partnership involving collaboration between national and regional governmental agencies and knowledge generation institutions (national and regional universities and regional science parks) and national and regional industry organisations. It should have links to national and regional organisations and clusters.
- The CMO should analyse and advise on the potential for new path development in advanced agriculture and biotechnology and food-for-the-future in Chiang Mai and Chiang Rai and help agree relevant support actions with government, research and business. This should include development of a shared strategy document for the cluster.
- Introduce direct cluster development projects for advanced agriculture and biotechnology and food-for-the-future based on long-term funding. The CMO should identify and recruit potential start-up and scale-up firms to participate in these projects. The funded projects should include:
    - R&D collaborations involving groups of potential and existing start-ups and scale-ups working with universities, science parks and research organisations.
    - Workforce training projects for potential and existing start-ups and scale-ups.
    - Intensive business development services to potential and existing start-ups and scale-ups.
- In addition, the CMO should undertake activities to attract FDI and promote FDI-SME linkages (as discussed in chapter 4).
- The Chiang Mai and Chiang Rai cluster initiative should be a pilot. Further regional CMOs and cluster development projects should be created in other sectors and regions building on the experience of Chiang Mai and Chiang Rai.
- A national network of CMOs should be established to promote information exchange and capacity building on cluster development approaches as well as to create relevant linkages for SMEs and research organisations across sectors and regions. The national network should include an educational programme on cluster governance run by the regional science parks as well as a mobility scheme for CMO staff to move between CMOs.

References

Asheim, B. T. (2000), "Industrial Districts", in Clark, G., M. Feldman, and M. Gertler (eds), The Oxford Handbook of Economic Geography, Oxford University Press, Oxford, 413-431.

Asheim, B.T., M. Grillitsch and M. Trippl (2017), "Introduction: Combinatorial Knowledge Bases, Regional Innovation, and Development Dynamics", *Economic Geography*, 93(5): 429-435.

Benneworth, P., L. Coenen, J. Moodysson, and B.T. Asheim (2009), "Exploring the Multiple Roles of Lund University in Strengthening the Scania Regional Innovation System: Towards Institutional Learning?", *European Planning Studies*, 17(11): 1645-1664.

Chesbrough, H. (2003), Open Innovation, Harvard Business School Press: Boston.

Grillitsch, M. (2018), "Place-based entrepreneurship and innovation policy for industrial diversification", Papers in Innovation Studies, No. 2018/3, CIRCLE, Lund University.

Grillitsch, M., B. T. Asheim, and M. Trippl (2018), "Unrelated knowledge combinations: the unexplored potential for regional industrial path development". *Cambridge Journal of Regions, Economy and Society*, 11: 257-274.

Isaksen, A. and M. Trippl (2016), "Path Development in Different Regional Innovation Systems", 66-84, in M. Parrilli; R. Fitjar; and A. Rodríguez-Pose (eds.), Innovation Drivers and Regional Innovation Strategies, Routledge: New York and London.

Lagnevik, M., I. Sjöholm, A. Lareke, and J. Östberg (2003), The Dynamics of Innovation Clusters: A study of the Food Industry, Edward Elgar, Cheltenham, UK

OECD (2011), Thailand: Key Issues and Policies. OECD Studies on SMEs and Entrepreneurship. OECD Publishing, Paris.

Porter, M. (1990), The Competitive Advantage of Nations, Macmillan, London.

Porter, M. (1998), "Clusters and the new economics of competition", Harvard Business Review, November-December, 77-90.

Porter, M. (2000) "Locations, clusters and company strategy", in Clark, G., M. Feldman, and M. Gertler (eds.), The Oxford Handbook of Economic Geography, Oxford University Press, Oxford, 253-274.

Zukauskaite, E. and J. Moodysson (2016), "Multiple paths of development: knowledge bases and institutional characteristics of the Swedish food sector", *European Planning Studies*, 24: 589-606.

Notes

[1] A 'functional food' is defined as food with added ingredients for which scientific evidence of positive health effects can be demonstrated. In other words, it is a hybrid form between nutrition and a pharmaceutical.

[2] Although Food Innopolis belongs to the Super Cluster category, the tax and non- tax incentives are the same as for firms in Thailand Food Valley, as agriculture and biotechnology is only defined as a 'first S-curve' sector. For industries defined as 'future industries' and belonging to the 'new S-curve' industries, a 10-15 years corporate income tax exemption as well as a personal income tax exemption for international specialists to work in the specified areas are under consideration by the Ministry of Finance.

[3] Research from Norway shows that three times as many firms with deficit apply for a similar tax exemption as firms with a surplus. Thus, in Norway a cash reimbursement scheme is applied to make this incentive interesting for start-ups and scale-ups that have not yet generated a surplus.

www.ingramcontent.com/pod-product-compliance
Ingram Content Group UK Ltd.
Pitfield, Milton Keynes, MK11 3LW, UK
UKHW051505290926
15471UKWH00008B/1423

9 789264 744851